Use of Force:
Current Practice and Policy

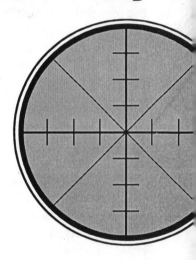

Craig Hemmens, J.D., Ph.D.

Eugene Atherton, Warden

American Correctional Association
Lanham, Maryland

FOUNDED 1870

Printed in the United States of America by Graphic Communications, Inc.,
    Upper Marlboro, Maryland.

ISBN 1-56991-098-7

This publication may be ordered from:
American Correctional Association
4380 Forbes Boulevard
Lanham, Maryland 20706-4322
1-800-222-5646

For information on publications and videos available from ACA, contact our worldwide web home page at: http://www.corrections.com/aca.

Library of Congress Cataloging-in-Publication Data

Hemmens, Craig.
    Use of force : current practice and policy / Craig Hemmens.
        p. cm.
    Includes bibliographical references.
    ISBN 1-56991-098-7
    1. Prison discipline—United States. 2. Restraint of prisoners-
    -United States. 3. Inmate guards—United States. 4. Correctional
    Law—United States. I. Title.
    HV9469.H44 1999
    365'.643—dc21   99-13336
                                                              CIP

Table of Contents

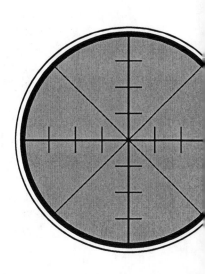

Foreword

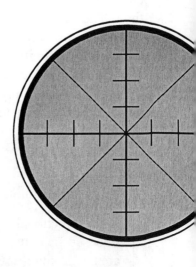

Fewer things raise more concern than the proper use of force in corrections. Yet, what is proper in one situation may not be so in another. In this work, Dr. Craig Hemmens who has a background in both corrections and law has teamed up with Eugene Atherton, a Colorado warden, who has extensive security experience, to provide guidance to the field. The initial publication was based on a survey sent to each of the state departments of correction and to large jails. Then, based on the answers to the survey, the authors added relevant material and provided samples of various types of policies and procedures that others may decide to adapt to their own situations.

The suggestions in this work also are in keeping with the American Correctional Association (ACA) standards on self-defense; training; security and control; weapons, restraints, and other security devices; as well as additional areas. The general principle in the standards is that "the institution uses a combination of supervision, inspection, accountability, and clearly defined policies and procedures on use of weapons and force to promote safe and orderly operations." ACA's standards manuals provide guidance on how to accomplish this.

ACA initially passed its policy on use of force at its Orlando conference in 1985 and it has been reviewed and left unchanged twice since then. The latest review was January, 1995 at the Winter Conference in Dallas, Texas. This use-of-force policy is important because it provides the framework for understanding the major concerns and ethical responses that the use of force in correctional settings provokes. ACA advocates that in most instances, only the proper amount of force be used—whether it is talking with an inmate, using a SWAT team to excavate a cell, or using other alternatives that often are grouped around a continuum.

ACA's Public Correctional Policy on Use of Force

Correctional agencies administer sanctions and punishments imposed by courts for unlawful behavior. Assigned to correctional agencies involuntarily, offenders sometimes resist authority imposed on them, and may demonstrate violent and destructive behaviors. Use of legally authorized force by correctional authorities may become necessary to maintain custody, safety, and control.

Use of force consists of physical contact with an offender in a confrontational situation to control behavior and enforce order. Use of force includes use of restraints (other than for routine transportation and movement), chemical agents, and weapons. Force is justified only when required to maintain or regain control, or when there is imminent danger of personal injury or serious damage to property. To ensure the use of force is appropriate and justifiable, correctional agencies should:

- Establish and maintain policies that require reasonable steps be taken to reduce or prevent the necessity for the use of force, that authorize force only when no reasonable alternative is possible, that permit only the minimum force necessary, and that prohibit the use of force as a retaliatory or disciplinary measure.

- Establish and enforce procedures that define the range of methods for and alternatives to the use of force, and that specify the conditions under which each is permitted. The procedures must assign responsibility for authorizing such force and ensure appropriate documentation and supervision of the action;

- Establish and maintain procedures that limit the use of deadly force to those instances where it is legally authorized and where there is an imminent threat to human life or a threat to public safety that cannot reasonably be prevented by other means;

- Maintain operating procedures and regular staff training designed to anticipate, stabilize, and diffuse situations that might give rise to conflict, confrontation, and violence;

- Provide specialized training to ensure competency in all methods of use of force, especially in methods and equipment requiring special knowledge and skills such as defensive tactics, weapons, restraints and chemical agents; and

- Establish and maintain procedures that require all incidents involving the use of force be fully documented and independently reviewed by a higher correctional authority. A report of the use of force, including appropriate investigation and any recommendations for preventive and remedial action, shall be submitted for administrative review and implementation of recommendations when appropriate."

Thus, based on the ACA's policy and standards, legal findings, and survey responses, we are pleased to provide some constructive suggestions for handling use of force incidents. This book is a significant addition to the literature available to the corrections field.

James A. Gondles, Jr.
Executive Director
American Correctional Association

Acknowledgments

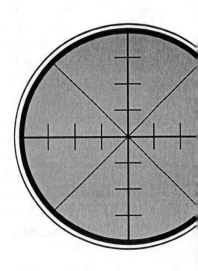

We would like to thank all the individuals in corrections departments, jails, and juvenile facilities who participated in the survey of correctional use of force. We would be remiss if we did not thank all of those who helped in the writing of this book. In particular, we thank the corrections departments and the individuals in those departments who took the time to respond to the survey conducted as part of this research. We asked for a lot of information, not all of which was easily accessible to corrections departments. Yet, we received a tremendous response, not only to our survey, but to our request for any additional information that corrections departments might have. We also thank those individuals who contributed to the chapter on current use of force policies. They were selected for their special contributions as correctional professionals

Acknowledgments

throughout their careers. They all have operated in the public corrections arena and have operated as private consultants. Each one has had significant experience in the development and operation of the use of force programs across the country. We deeply appreciate that they took time out from their important schedules to contribute. Their efforts have provided a richness of thought throughout the book. It is important also to thank the corrections staff at Colorado State Penitentiary for their encouragement and support in producing this book. Your willingness to share information with others in the field demonstrates the highest degree of professionalism.

We would also like to thank our contributing authors. Darrell Ross contributed a chapter on policy implementation. Jeff Maahs and Travis Pratt assisted with the statistical analysis, and the chapter on the history of the use of force in corrections. Obviously this book could not have come into existence without their able assistance.

Craig Hemmens would like to acknowledge Professors Rolando V. del Carmen and James W. Marquart of Sam Houston State University, the two men most responsible for his professional development. What I do right can be attributed to them; what I do wrong is my fault alone. I should have listened more closely! I would also like to acknowledge the contributions made by my colleague and wife, Mary K. Stohr, to both my professional and personal development. She makes it all worthwhile. Thanks also to Emily Stohr-Gilmore, who has helped me more than she will ever know.

The person most responsible for this book, however, is Alice Fins of the American Correctional Association. She persuaded the first author to undertake the project, and pushed him along ever so gently to completion. We thank her for her faith in us and the project.

Eugene Atherton wishes to thank the following contributors:

Joan Palmateer, Warden
Oregon State Penitentiary
Oregon Department of Corrections

Jerry Gasko, Deputy Director of Prisons
Colorado Department of Corrections

Dr. Joseph Abramajtys, Warden
Muskegon Regional Correctional Facility
Vice President, Integrated Management and Treatment Systems

Richard Franklin, Program Specialist
Prison Security Programs
National Institute of Corrections

Larry Cothran, Chairman
Technology Transfer Committee
California Department of Corrections

Stan Czerniak, Assistant Secretary for Security and
    Institutional Management
Florida Department of Corrections

Dr. Jeffery Schwartz
LETRA, Inc.
Campbell, California

Introduction

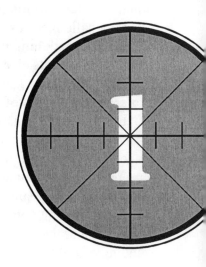

During the past quarter century, corrections has faced a number of challenges. Many of these challenges have come from outside the institution walls, as the public and courts have become more involved in the operation and management of correctional institutions. New laws and court decisions have limited the discretion and independence of corrections departments. The inmate population has changed, as increasing numbers of minorities and drug offenders are sent to prison, often for long periods. A large number of offenders come to prison with a history of violence.

Corrections departments have responded to these challenges by drastically changing the way institutions are operated. The quality of corrections personnel has been improved, as new training standards have been implemented and departments have modified and clarified operating policies. One unfortunate result has been a tremendous increase in paperwork and bureaucracy, as departments seek to meet current standards and to provide documentation of their actions in the event of a legal challenge. A positive result has been the creation and promulgation of professional standards by a number of organizations, including the American Correctional Association.

As public and judicial awareness of corrections has increased, correctional administrators have been forced to make changes to institutional policies. No longer are the actions of corrections personnel likely to go unchallenged. Courts have become more willing to consider claims of inmates, and inmates have responded by filing an ever-increasing number of lawsuits challenging virtually every aspect of institutional life, from the type of food served to the right to exercise their religious beliefs, and other conditions of confinement.

Inmate litigation has become one of the primary forces for change in correctional policies and procedures, as corrections departments either make changes to comply with a court decision (the reactive approach), or alter procedures to avoid possible litigation (the proactive approach). The majority of inmate suits target prison administrators and correctional officers, and seek monetary damages. Thus, it is clearly important, for the individual and the organization, to have a clear and comprehensive understanding of policies and procedures that can reduce or eliminate liability.

One area that remains in the spotlight is the use of force by corrections personnel. Incarceration, by its nature, involves forcing an individual to do something against his or her will. Not surprisingly, these incarcerated individuals are sometimes uncooperative, sometimes to the point of physical resistance.

Corrections officers have the right and responsibility to use reasonable force to protect themselves and others, and to insure compliance with institutional policies. Additionally, while correctional officers have the right and duty to use force in certain circumstances, it is also true that every individual has a right to be free from offensive bodily contact. It is true that inmates lose many rights when they are incarcerated, but they do not shed all of their constitutional rights at the prison door. Freedom from unwarranted attack by other inmates or correctional staff is one of these rights.

What is reasonable in one situation may not be in another. The type and amount of force that are appropriate are subject to debate. As new technology is developed (such as electronic stun guns and mobile restraint devices), issues arise as to the applicability of this technology to the correctional setting.

The question in prison is not *whether* force can be used, but rather *when* force can be used, and *how much* force can be used? These are two tougher questions, and they can be answered only by looking at what the courts say and what prisons do. In this book, we present an overview of the law regarding use of force and a summary of current use-of-force policies.

This book is intended primarily for use by correctional officers and administrators interested in learning more about the use of force in corrections. It describes, in a general fashion, the history of, legal issues involving, and current policies on the use of force in corrections. It is written in a straightforward, nonlegalistic style. Chapter 1 is an introduction and overview of the subject. Chapter 2 offers a brief historical background on the use of force in corrections. Chapter 3 contributes to the discussion of the legal issues surrounding the use of force in corrections, including both deadly and nondeadly force. Chapter 4 describes a national survey of correctional use of force policies and procedures and provides several model policies. Chapter 5 contains a summary and description of current use of force techniques and practices. Chapter 6 shows how to create and implement an effective use-of-force policy. Finally, Chapter 7 provides a summary and conclusion. Included in the references are a bibliography for additional reading, several sample use-of-force policies and forms, and a copy of the national survey sent to corrections departments.

This book is intended for a wide audience, both within and outside the corrections field. We hope that correctional personnel, from newly hired line officers to seasoned administrators, will benefit from the discussion which follows. Those not working in corrections also can benefit from learning how corrections departments deal with the troubling issue of use of force, and why corrections departments do what they do.

This book is for all who work in corrections; it would not have been possible without their aid.

The Role of the Correctional Officer

Correctional officers are responsible for performing a variety of tasks. They supervise those individuals sentenced to prison. They maintain institutional security and safety, maintain order, enforce rules and regulations, and perform a number of other tasks, depending on their position and the type of institution in which they work. Correctional officers spend much of their time monitoring the activities of inmates. To maintain institutional order and security, correctional officers frequently are involved in searching for contraband, maintaining discipline, settling disputes, and engaging in conflict resolution.

Professional correctional officers are well aware that their job is much more complex than simply ensuring inmates remain inside the prison walls. Line officers are responsible for the supervision of inmates in a variety of settings and tasks. These inmates often are angry and/or emotionally on edge as a result of their confinement, and they are likely to have a history of not handling conflict well. Correctional officers frequently are called on to resolve conflicts which arise when tempers flare. Acts that might be meaningless in the free world take on an entirely different meaning behind prison walls. Correctional officers often have a tendency to view their relations with inmates in an adversarial context: "us versus them."

There are a number of ways to reduce the potential for conflict, and to manage conflict when it does occur. Techniques include avoidance, accommodation, compromise, and confrontation (Christian, 1999). Conflict management operates on the premise that both sides can be satisfied with the outcome of a situation only if each feels he or she has been treated fairly. This requires cooperation and collaboration.

One of the inevitable results of performing the duties of a correctional officer is that officers infrequently are called on to use force against an inmate, either in self-defense, or in defense of others, for protection of property, or to maintain institutional security and order. Consequently, a concern with being assaulted by an inmate is part of the mindset of a correctional officer (Kratcoski, 1987; Morris and Morris, 1980). Much of the literature on inmate violence and inmate assaults on correctional officers suggests it is related to three factors: facility crowding, inmate age, and prisonization effects (Ekland-Olsen, et al., 1983,

---

4

Kratcoski, 1987; Marquart, 1986). Some experts suggest that inmate assaults on correctional officers may be based in part on both officers and inmates acting towards each other based on stereotypical images. Both sides think the other is prone to violence, and interaction between the two is based on this perception (Lombardo, 1982).

Between 1990 and 1995, assaults on correctional staff by inmates grew a third, from 10,731 in 1990 to 14,165 in 1995 (Stephan, 1997). While much of this increase can be explained by a combination of factors, including the sudden, dramatic increase in the number of individuals incarcerated, the imposition of longer sentences, and prison crowding, it indicates that violence towards correctional officers is still a major issue in corrections.

While inmate-on-staff assaults long have been a problem, few studies of assaults on correctional officers have been conducted. In an early study, Bowker (1980) found that most assaults on correctional officers occurred either as unexpected attacks or as patterned spontaneous attacks. Planned attacks tended to occur when officers were conducting routine, everyday tasks in risk-prone areas. Unexpected attacks occurred largely in a random and unpredictable pattern.

One study of assaults on correctional officers in a federal institution and a state institution found that in the federal institution, the majority 57 percent of assaults were classified as "minor," involving conduct such as spitting, shoving, throwing liquid substances or other nondangerous items. Forty-three percent of the assaults were classified as "serious," involving striking an officer with an object that could do physical injury, and where pain/threat of serious injury were present. In the state institution, 32 percent of the assaults were classified as minor while 78 percent of the assaults were classified as serious (Kratcoski, 1987).

Most of the assaults in both facilities occurred in either the cellblock area or the administrative segregation area. However, most of the assaults in the administrative segregation area were minor, while most of the serious assaults occurred in the housing areas. This is explained by the fact that the administrative segregation unit inmates were largely unable to come into direct contact with the correctional officers, being locked in their cells for extended periods of time, and so were largely restricted to throwing things at the officers.

The study also found that officers with less than one year of experience were more likely to be assaulted, and that most assaults occurred without any physical or verbal warning from the inmate.

Another study of assaults on correctional officers, in New York, found that assaults occur for a variety of reasons, and in a number of contexts. Only 2 percent of the inmates were reported to have assaulted an officer—a clear minority. Most assaults (82 percent) occurred in maximum-security prisons. Ninety-seven percent of all assaults involved an inmate acting alone. Almost half of the assaults occurred in general population housing areas, while another 24 percent occurred in a special housing area, such as administrative segregation. Seventy-seven percent of the assaults did not involve the use of a weapon. Assaultive inmates tended to be younger than nonassaultive inmates. Twenty-six percent of the assaults were unexplained, 13 percent occurred after the inmate refused an officer's command, 11 percent occurred as protest over what the inmate considered unfair treatment, and 10 percent occurred while inmates were fighting among themselves and officers intervened. The data for this research was collected from the correctional officer's incident reports (Light, 1991).

A national survey of assaults on correctional officers found that more than 80 percent of assaults occurred in maximum-custody institutions. Seventy-four percent of the assaults occurred in the housing units. Of these, 46 percent occurred in general population housing units, and 28 percent took place in special housing units, such as administrative segregation. More than 70 percent of the inmates involved in assaults were serving sentences for either murder, aggravated assault, armed robbery, or robbery. Of these attacks, 63 percent involved physical contact and 29 percent involved throwing (or spitting) objects or liquids. Slightly more than 22 percent of the assaults occurred while correctional officers were enforcing institutional rules, 21 percent occurred while the officer was giving orders to an inmate, and 18 percent occurred while the officer was supervising inmates (Ross, 1985).

A recent study of inmate assaults on staff in maximum-security prisons revealed that the gender of the correctional officer is related to the likelihood of assault. While the presence of women as correctional officers has been criticized in the past, more women than ever before are entering the corrections field. And while traditional thinking was that female officers would be at greater risk of assault due to their gender and smaller physical size, this research indicates that, in fact, female officers are less likely to be attacked by an inmate. This research was conducted at maximum-security prisons in seven different states in 1992, and the researcher found that male officers were assaulted 3.6 times more often than female officers (Rowan, 1996).

The research on inmate-on-staff assaults indicates many assaults are triggered by officers just doing their job—performing routine tasks such as enforcing institutional rules, breaking up fights, and supervising inmates. These findings suggest a correctional officer cannot always predict or prevent inmate assaults. Often, it appears that inmates simply reach their boiling point, and take their anger out on the nearest symbol of authority—the correctional officer.

Use of Force in Corrections

Physical confrontations between correctional officer and inmate are part of the reality of prison life. Because of the potentially serious consequences of these conflicts, use of force issues continue to be a critical issue in corrections. Working in a correctional institution is a dangerous job, a job in which correctional officers are called on to make split-second judgments, which have long-term consequences.

The use of force against inmates is a necessary, if unfortunate, part of the job of the correctional officer. Correctional personnel are charged with maintaining institutional safety and security, insuring compliance with institutional rules and regulations, and protecting inmates, staff, and visitors. While the majority of inmates generally follow the rules and comply with the requests of correctional officers, a minority refuse to cooperate or obey the rules, or they attack another inmate or a correctional officer. They may do so for a variety of reasons. Regardless of the reason for this, the correctional officer may have to resort to force to regain control of the situation. Additionally, a correctional officer's attitude, demeanor, or approach to a particular situation may determine whether force is used.

Correctional officers are permitted to use force, so long as they do so "reasonably." But what is reasonable? The answer is, it depends. It depends on the particular situation. The courts have laid down basic, minimal guidelines for what constitutes the appropriate degree of force. Various organizations such as the American Correctional Association, have promulgated model policies. The American Correctional Association's *Standards for Adult Correctional Institutions* (1990) includes the following policy for use of force:

> Written policy, procedure and practice restrict the use of physical force to instances of justifiable self-defense, protection of others, protection of property, and prevention of escapes, and then only as a last resort and in accordance with appropriate statutory authority. In no event is physical force justifiable as punishment. A written report is prepared following all uses of force and is submitted to administrative staff for review (Use of Force 3-4198, 1990).

Correctional policies and procedures of individual departments and institutions provide further guidance. These vary in specificity. An example is the policy of the Federal Bureau of Prisons:

> The Bureau of Prisons authorizes staff to use force only as a last alternative after all other reasonable efforts to resolve a situation have failed. When authorized, staff must use only that amount of force necessary to gain control of the inmate; to protect and ensure the safety of inmates, staff, and others; to prevent serious property damage; and to ensure institution security and good order (#5566.04, 1997)

Correctional departments in most jurisdictions provide training not only on how to use force, but also on how much force to use in particular situations, and when not to use force at all, as well as how to avoid use of force through interpersonal communication.

In this book, we discuss the basic legal requirements involving the use of force in corrections, and also provide a summary of current use of force policies employed in various state departments of correction. All correctional officers are strongly advised to familiarize themselves with the use of force policies in place in their department and institution, as every policy is a little different. Some policies are very concise, perhaps consisting of just a few paragraphs, while others may be several pages long. Some policies give only the most generalized guidance; others are very specific and attempt to address every situation, which may arise. Some policies discuss only when and how much force is appropriate; others discuss these issues as well as how to resolve situations without resorting to force.

There is no one "perfect" policy that applies to all situations and all places. By comparing different policies, and by seeing what other departments consider important issues, each individual and each department can learn from the wisdom and experience of the others.

The Role of Institutional Policies

As previously mentioned, corrections agencies have responded to court intervention and changing public perceptions of the proper way to run a prison by modifying existing policies, or, in many cases, creating new policies. The result, for the correctional officer, is that a job that once involved little paperwork and minimal administrative oversight is now awash in policies, paperwork, and multiple levels of administrative review.

Policies and rules are an important part of any organization, including correctional institutions. Policies are general statements of principles and objectives in a particular area. A policy is a statement of what is to be done in relation to a certain issue, and is intended to shape attitude (Drapkin, 1996).

A rule is much more specific than a policy. A rule spells out more precisely how a policy is to be accomplished—rules detail what is to be done or not done in specific situations. It is intended to shape behavior (Drapkin, 1996).

Institutional and departmental policies can serve as both the bane and the savior of the correctional line officer, however. While learning and interpreting policies is an arduous task, the policies serve several important functions. These include the following:

- Providing information to the line officer

- Providing guidance to the line officer

- Providing a defense to inmate lawsuits for the line officer

- Promoting professionalism and consistency within the organization

- Providing a foundation for training new staff and retraining for current staff

Policies provide correctional officers with information about how to do their job. While most correctional officers receive a degree of training before beginning their job and some receive in-service training, this is often in the form of lectures and demonstrations. Written policies provide a reference point for officers, one they can return to throughout their career.

Policies also provide correctional officers with guidance. They set forth the "rules" by which correctional officers are expected to perform their job, and they give officers some idea of what is expected of them. New staff are often uncertain of their role in prison, and legal developments, which the seasoned officer is unaware of, may occur. Policies which reflect current legal requirements provide rookie and experienced officers alike with direction and serve to reduce confusion.

Policies also provide correctional officers (and the institution) with some protection from liability. Assuming the policies are based on legal standards of conduct (discussed in Chapter 3), actions by correctional officers that are in accord with these policies are likely to be upheld by courts if challenged by inmate plaintiffs. Virtually every action taken by a correctional officer or administrator has potential legal implications. Certainly, any time that force is used on an inmate, legal liability may arise. Thus, it is essential that all personnel have access to the best, most complete, and most understandable knowledge and guidance regarding how and when to use force.

According to one prominent psychologist, excessive use of force by correctional officers is based on correctional officer subcultural norms supporting violence against inmates. This feeling is based on correctional officer's fear and mistrust of inmates and the inability of officers to establish meaningful relationships with inmates, so they fail to see them as human beings (Toch, 1977).

One study found that use of force is in part a function of the organizational structure of the institution. According to a study conducted in

Texas, laxity on the part of the administration in enforcing correctional officer compliance with policies and procedures creates a culture in which individual officers are allowed, even encouraged, to control situations as they see fit. In this situation, correctional officers were more likely to use force as a means of control (Marquart, 1986). Changing the culture of a large institution or bureaucracy is very difficult, as subcultural norms become engrained and resistance to change is entrenched.

Correctional standards were created in an attempt to provide guidelines for the minimal level of care mandated by law, and that is in accord with professional ethics. Several different standards are put forth by various organizations, but all share this common goal—the bare minimum required of a correctional institution. Whether a prison system goes beyond this level is up to prison administrators who are working under the twin dilemmas of tight budgets and popular resentment of criminals. Proponents of the principle of less eligibility believe the treatment accorded an inmate should not be superior to that provided a member of the lowest social class in the free society (Sieh, 1989).

According to the U.S. Supreme Court, corrections administrators provide all the care they are required by law to provide so long as they do not manifest "deliberate indifference" to the needs of inmates. This is something akin to recklessness, and it is a relatively modest standard to meet. There is little demand from the public to provide inmates with anything more than the bare minimum. Additionally, corrections budgets are stretched to the breaking point, and security and safety remain paramount concerns of most administrators.

Also, as the inmate population changes, corrections must adjust to this shift in the type of offenders and number of inmates. With this new and growing population, now is the time to address the adequacy of correctional use-of-force policies and procedures. Corrections departments all have use-of-force policies, in one form or another. These policies no longer may be adequate, however, given the changing face of corrections. Furthermore, general standards do not provide, and cannot provide, all the answers. Standards show what *must* be done—they do not necessarily show what *ought* to be done. It is here that complete, well-thought-out policies and procedures on the use of force come into play.

The History of the Use of Force in Corrections

Travis Pratt

Jeffrey Maahs

Craig Hemmens

Introduction

This chapter provides a historical context for a discussion of the use in force in corrections today. It is not a general history of corrections; that is something that has been dealt with by others (Keve, 1991; Roberts, 1997; Morris and Rothman, 1995). The first part of the chapter traces the use of force from its early roots, through English common law, to the present conception of the "proper" use of force in the correctional setting. The second part of the chapter discusses the movement of the federal courts from a "hands-off" position toward inmate cases, where prison officials were free to operate their facilities without any external legal oversight, to one of judicial intervention. The chapter concludes with a discussion of the movement towards the adoption of correctional standards, which provide guidance to correctional officers seeking to understand when and how to use force.

Use of Force in Early Times

Throughout history, the use of force, most often through the imposition of punishment, has taken many forms. The reader should recognize that "nonlegal" punishment was practiced long before the "legal" use of force was ever developed (Newman, 1985). Prior to the advent of written legal codes, the victim (or general public) was largely responsible for the punishment of the offender. Examples include stoning in the biblical period (3000 B.C. to A.D. 500), and blood feuds during the medieval era (A.D. 500-1000).

From the end of the middle ages through the early modern period in England and western Europe (roughly the late 1600s), punishment became more formalized and ceremonial (Johnson, 1990). Specifically, certain procedures began to develop for using force against offenders that made the process of punishment less erratic and more routinized. Given that American guidelines surrounding use of force policies in corrections are rooted in the English experience, it is important to examine the development of punishment during this period in England.

The use of force in early modern England was corporal, public, and carried out by the state. Common punishments included mutilating, branding, whipping, and torturing. These punishments most often were public displays aimed at the education of the citizenry (Radzinowicz, 1948). Thus, punishment efforts were to be carefully staged, proper, and dignified undertakings (Atholl, 1954). With regard to public executions, Johnson (1990) notes that:

> English citizens, including school children, were encouraged to observe the condemned in their cells (the prisoners were exhibited for this purpose) and to attend [executions] to see firsthand the fate of those who had gone bad and therefore "come to a bad end"—the end of a rope.

While education of the public was the reason for public executions, it appears these events often served as a form of public entertainment, as citizens would attend the executions and engage in celebrations prior to the execution (Marquart, et al., 1994). Regardless of its form or stated intent, however, after the late 1600s, the English tradition (as well as the rest of continental Europe) placed the authority over the use of force in the hands of the state.

Use of Force in Common Law

Until the late 1600s, punishment was delivered by both the monarch and the church; each maintained authority over separate domains of criminal behavior. In the wake of the division of religious and civic (political) authority in England (where a breakdown occurred in the belief that the monarch was granted his or her political power from God), John Locke's notions of individual rights and the "social contract" gathered considerable momentum.

Locke argued that the authority to govern was created through collective agreement between the government and the governed (a social contract) and that the state should exist only to protect the "natural rights" of individuals (Locke, 1980 [1690]). As such, the state's mandate was to prevent individuals from arbitrarily exercising coercive force over one another; thus, the state should, as a matter of law, have sole control over the use of force. This "social contract" perspective shaped the common law development of the authority over the use of force in England, which, in turn, influenced the rest of western Europe and the United States (Weber, 1947).

The American Experience

The use of force in the early American period (up until the mid-1800s) was largely based on the English model of punishment: for the stated purpose of retribution. Whether viewed through the lens of *lex talionis* (the doctrine of an "eye for an eye"), or the current language of "deserved punishment," retribution suggests that the punishment is necessary simply to balance the scales of justice (Newman, 1985; *see also* Kant, 1965 [1787]). During this early American period (1650-1830), the form of the punishment remained, as in England, public and corporal—prison rarely was used as an instrument of punishment.

This model of criminal justice eventually was replaced, however, by the rise of the utilitarian philosophical tradition in the 1800s. Utilitarian philosophy held that punishment should not be an end in and of itself (as it is in retribution or revenge), but rather punishment should be used as a means of achieving a larger goal, such as controlling criminal behavior (Beccaria, 1963 [1764]; Bentham, 1970 [1789]).

For example, Beccaria's (1963 [1764]) utilitarian theory of the relationship between punishment and crime, "deterrence," can be summarized as follows: crime should decrease as the swiftness, certainty, and severity of punishments increase. Given this assumption, he advocated a system where the severity of punishments should be slightly greater than the severity of the crime. While this "theory" may sound rather simple now, it was a radical departure from the conventional wisdom of the past. The implementation of this more "enlightened" view of crime and punishment required a more rational approach to the use of force against the offender. Accordingly, punishment practices at this time became less visible to the public.

From Public Punishment to the Prison

Beginning in the mid-1800s, antiquated forms of public corporal punishment—such as beheading, stoning, public hanging, breaking on the wheel, engaging in live burials, drowning, putting individuals in stocks and pillories, burning, and quartering—lost their public appeal.

The development of the prison as a means of punishment and social control was a natural outgrowth of Americans' understanding of the causes of deviance. The prison, or penitentiary, was created to remove the "dangerous classes" from society and to provide them with the opportunity (solitary confinement) to reflect on their misdeeds (Rothman, 1971). The penitentiary movement began with the opening of Auburn Prison in New York and Eastern Penitentiary in Pennsylvania.

As a replacement to the almshouses, poorhouses, and mental hospitals of the early nineteenth century, the prison became the primary institution where the use of force for punishment purposes took place (Staples, 1990). Despite the shift from public view to private incarceration, corporal punishment was still very much a part of corrections. As used here, the term *corporal punishment* refers to the infliction of physical pain on an inmate for discipline or restraint.

Now hidden from public view and, therefore somewhat immune from public accountability, prison officials routinely inflicted a variety of corporal punishments on inmates. Examples included flogging inmates with a rawhide whip, or a "cat" made of wire strands, and physical beatings (Inciardi, 1990). Use of solitary confinement, or the "hole" also became common.

Although many states officially prohibited corporal punishment by 1900, Delaware's prisons employed whipping until 1954, and the law sanctioning it remained on the books until 1972 (Rothman, 1995). In addition, Arkansas openly used corporal punishment (including electrical shocking devices) until the 1960s (Palmer, 1997). While many states currently have no statute explicitly prohibiting corporal punishments in prison, the practice is forbidden by most corrections departments and corrections standards, and the few courts that have addressed the issues have been clear (since the late 1960s) in rejecting any corporal punishment as legitimate.

Thus, punishment (and use of force) has evolved over the last few centuries in the following manner:

1. Private revenge, carried out by the victim in the middle ages

2. Public, state-sanctioned corporal punishment (1600s-1800s)

3. Nonpublic, state-sanctioned prison sentences that included corporal punishment (1800s to 1960s)

4. Nonpublic, state sanction of prison (1960-present)

The purpose of punishment also has changed over time, from revenge, to deterrence, to rehabilitation. Current goals of corrections include all of these, as well as "incapacitation," which simply means confining offenders to limit their opportunity to further victimize society.

Despite the plurality of positions regarding what the overriding goal of corrections should be, there is a consensus that corporal punishment is not a legitimate practice in modern penology. That is, the punishment aspect of prison is the deprivation of liberty, and further punishment is not necessary. Even so, the revival of practices such as "chain gangs," which mirror the prison labor practices of the early 1900s, indicates that the use of force in corrections has not fully broken away from its common law/corporal punishment roots.

Chain gangs frequently were used by corrections departments after the Civil War and during the early part of the twentieth century. They involved using inmates as laborers outside the prison. While the inmates were outside the prison, they were chained together as a means both of preventing their escape and punishing them physically and emotionally. In recent years, several states have experimented with using chain gangs again, expressly for the purpose of "shaming" prisoners.

The Federal Courts—From "Hands-Off" to Intervention

Until the mid-1900s, prison administrators were given wide latitude to run prisons, with little political or judicial intervention (Jacobs, 1977). Although state courts heard a few scattered inmate cases, federal courts maintained a "hands-off" policy with regard to all inmate issues, including the use of force by correctional officers, for at least two reasons.

First, the judiciary spurned prison cases out of concern for a separation of powers between the courts and executive decision makers. At the time, the separation of power between the judicial and executive branches of government precluded judicial intervention into any executive agency. Further, the courts argued that since they were not penologists, any intrusion into prison operations would disrupt prison officials' administrative efforts at maintaining internal security and inmate discipline.

Second, the courts also held that prisoners did not have the same rights as free citizens. This idea is summarized in *Ruffin v. Commonwealth* (1871):

> The prisoner has, as a consequence of his crime, not only forfeited his liberty, but all his personal rights except those which the law in its humanity accords to him. He is for the time being the slave of the state.

The idea that an inmate is a slave of the state began to lose favor in the mid-twentieth century. In 1944, the Sixth Circuit Court of Appeals held that an inmate retains all the rights of an ordinary, free citizen except those rights expressly taken from him by statute, or those which are, by necessary implication, limited by the fact of his incarceration (*Coffin v. Reichard*, 1944).

The limited view of inmate's rights, as well as the political and legal insulation enjoyed by prison officials, came under sustained attack in the 1960s. During this period, constitutional protections were extended to previously marginalized groups in society such as women, juveniles, and racial minorities in the areas of voting, housing, employment, education, and reproductive freedom. Eventually, this movement found its way to the correctional arena, with prisoners being viewed as another politically disenfranchised group. The U.S. Supreme Court, in its embrace of the 1960s civil rights movement, abandoned the "hands off" doctrine formerly associated with prisons in favor of a more "interventionist" approach.

The end of hands-off era was clearly signaled by *Cooper v. Pate* (1964). In this case, the U.S. Supreme Court ruled that inmates in state and local correctional institutions are entitled to protection against violations of their constitutional rights. Specifically, the Court held that inmates could sue a warden, correctional officer, or other prison official for monetary damages under 42 U.S.C. 1983, a federal statute that imposes civil liability on any person who deprives another of constitutional rights.

The end of the hands-off period was a difficult one for correctional administrators and line staff. Correctional administrators suddenly were forced to open their institutions up to public and judicial scrutiny. They lost a great deal of their autonomy, as they had to answer to review boards and judges. Line staff suffered a loss of prestige, as the public, nurtured on only the gruesome headline-making cases such as the Arkansas prison scandal, came to perceive them as brutal and sadistic oppressors. Line officers also were forced to justify their treatment of inmates, and inmates were suddenly much more vocal in demanding better treatment.

Since the 1960s, the amount of inmate civil litigation has increased dramatically: from 216 inmate cases in 1968 to more than 40,000 (10 percent of the federal civil court docket) in 1996 (Maahs and del Carmen, 1995). Lawsuits filed encompass most inmate complaints, including poor living conditions, violations of religious freedom, denial of access to courts, unequal treatment, and, of course, unwarranted use of force by prison officials (Hansen and Daley, 1995). However, brief filings have dropped dramatically in recent years, since Congress passed the Prison Litigation Reform Act, which limits inmate lawsuits.

The Standards Movement

One of the first instances in which standards were discussed was during the Congress on Penitentiary and Reformatory Discipline in 1870. Conference attendees promulgated the first set of corrections standards, or as they titled the document, "Declaration of Principles." These principles covered the full range of prison operations. Unfortunately, the Declaration of Principles had virtually no impact on correctional operations.

Prior to the 1960s, America paid little attention to corrections. This began to change as the Attica prison riot and several well-publicized prison scandals focused public attention on prisons and courts became more receptive to inmate litigation. Prison administrators responded to the harsh criticism they received in part by attempting to professionalize the prison environment. Part of this movement to professionalize corrections was the development of professional standards.

In 1966, the American Correctional Association published an update of the 1870 Declaration of Principles, entitled *Standards for Correctional Institutions*. In 1968, correctional administrators responded to public and judicial pressure to improve prison conditions by creating a task force to develop standards for correctional institutions. In 1970, the Project on Self-Evaluation and Accreditation presented its findings at the annual Congress of Corrections. Little if any meaningful reform occurred, however (Hemmens, 1997).

Additionally, standards were driven by the need for efficiency in operations as systems grew to encompass a large array of facilities and thousands of staff. It became crucial to standardize language and approaches to basic operations across entire departments. Such changes, properly orchestrated, have brought many assets to contemporary corrections, including the following:

1. Operations staff no longer are distracted by the challenge of having to answer basic questions repeatedly throughout the operational year.

2. Standards have allowed operations staff to focus on issues of greater importance in managing day-to-day operations.

3. Standards have allowed staff to agree formally on basic tenets of operations with the opportunity for review and modification.

4. Standards have eliminated the need to depend heavily on leadership for answers to basic questions on a routine basis, a practice which consumes time and takes attention away from the daily tasks.

In eliminating this dependency, operations staff are empowered to focus on higher levels of performance. In addition, corrections systems that have successfully incorporated standards and standards management as a part of their operation usually can show trends of greater program performance, especially under increasingly more difficult demands.

During the 1970s, a number of organizations promulgated professional standards covering virtually every aspect of the prison environment (Keve, 1996). In 1974, the Commission on Accreditation for Corrections was established by the American Correctional Association, and in 1977, the American Correctional Association published a comprehensive set of standards for operating jails and prisons. These standards have been updated on a regular basis to the present.

The standards movement was a reaction to the growing professionalization of corrections and the increased judicial scrutiny of corrections. Today, standards play a large role in guiding correctional operations. In addition, institutions and entire departments have adopted comprehensive procedures and policies governing virtually every aspect of institutional life. Use-of-force situations are no exception. Current use-of-force policies are examined in Chapter 4. In Chapter 3, we present a discussion of the legal issues and standards involved, which affect the development of use-of-force policies.

Conclusion

Force is still an everyday occurrence in corrections. While force as a means of formal punishment (as in corporal punishment) has ceased, and official policies condoning the use of excessive force to punish and/or control recalcitrant inmates have been discarded, force as a means of informal punishment remains a concern. Recent litigation concerning treatment of inmates in Pelican Bay State Prison in California is an example (*Madrid v. Gomez*, 889 F. Supp. 1146 (N.D. Cal. 1995).

Legal Issues Involving Use of Force in Corrections

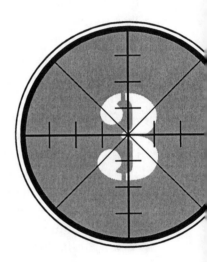

Introduction

This chapter examines the legal issues surrounding use of force in corrections, focusing on the Eighth Amendment prohibition on "cruel and unusual" punishment, and the different standards of review used by the courts in cases involving corrections. We also include a discussion of the basis for correctional officer liability.

The few U.S. Supreme Court cases involving use of force in corrections are discussed. Most Supreme Court decisions involving corrections have dealt with other issues, such as freedom of religion, due process, and general "conditions of confinement."

Furthermore, state tort law may apply to actions of corrections personnel. It is essential, therefore, that corrections personnel familiarize themselves with the laws of their respective states and the law as set forth by the U.S. Supreme Court. There are several excellent books, which cover correctional law in a comprehensive fashion; some are written for academics (Palmer, 1997), while others are written for corrections personnel (Collins, 1997). These references should be consulted for a comprehensive review of the law of corrections.

Correctional officers are not expected to be lawyers. However, they must be familiar with the legal standards of conduct as they apply in the prison setting if they are to be able to do a good job and avoid running afoul of the law. During the past quarter century, courts have become intimately involved with the operation of corrections facilities, and litigation has played a tremendous role in reshaping corrections policies and practices.

On conviction of a crime, those incarcerated forfeit many, but not all of their constitutional rights. Rather, inmates are entitled to limited rights. The justification for limiting the rights of inmates is based largely on legitimate penological interests (such as security and order) and the exigencies of confinement (the necessity to control contraband and regulate intercourse with others). Courts are not experts in prison administration, but they are the final word on the constitutionality of government action. Consequently, they are involved in ensuring that the constitutional rights of all, including inmates, are not violated. Courts do defer in large part to the wisdom of correctional administrators, but there must be some showing of a legitimate penological interest.

The Eighth Amendment and "Cruel and Unusual" Punishment

The Eighth Amendment prohibits "cruel and unusual" punishment. Exactly what is cruel and unusual has changed as society has evolved. The Court at various times has defined it as punishment that is disproportionate to the offense, punishment that "shocks the conscience," and punishment that is not in accord with "evolving standards of decency." The Supreme Court has applied the standard to a variety of situations in corrections, including the death penalty, corporal punishment, and the use of force to control inmates, protect other inmates, or to repel an assault by an inmate.

The courts have employed three main standards, or tests, to determine whether a punishment is cruel and unusual: (1) whether the punishment shocks the general conscience of a civilized society; (2) whether the punishment goes beyond legitimate penal aims; and (3) whether the punishment is unnecessarily cruel and unusual (Clear and Cole, 1997). "Cruel and unusual" has been interpreted in correctional use-of-force cases to mean the "unnecessary and wanton infliction of pain" (*Whitley v. Albers*, 1986).

Two things should be clear from these tests. First, they all are relatively vague and subject to much interpretation by the lower courts. Second, they are subject to change over time. What is common practice today may be "shocking or unconscionable" years from now. Certainly, the common practices of the early colonial times (drawing and quartering) would be shocking if attempted today.

Yet, the courts have moved beyond these general tests, and it is now relatively clear what constitutes unnecessary force by corrections officers. The courts have defined both the *situations* in which force is permitted, and (to a lesser extent) the *amount* of force that is proper.

The majority of inmate suits target prison administrators and correctional officers and seek monetary damages. Further, a review of inmate cases suggests that use-of-force cases are among the most costly of inmate suits, as they require extensive research and documentation (Maahs and del Carmen, 1995). Thus, the legal standards associated with the use of force are critical for both administrators and correctional officers to understand.

In general, every prisoner has the right to be free of both actual offensive bodily contact and the fear of offensive bodily contact (Palmer, 1997). However, what is "offensive" is determined not by the inmate, but by the situation, and correctional officers have the right to use force to ensure legitimate penological interests, such as safety, order, and security. Prison officials are permitted to use reasonable force to enforce discipline and to protect themselves and others (*Whitley v. Albers*, 1986). The key here is that the force must be reasonable under the circumstances. Thus, prison officials may be justified in using extreme force, even deadly force, but only if the situation warrants it. In addition, the Supreme Court has held that correctional personnel may be liable for failing to prevent harm to an inmate by another inmate, but only if it can be demonstrated that their conduct displayed "deliberate indifference" to the safety of the inmate (*Farmer v. Brennan,* 1994).

Corporal Punishment

Corporal punishment once was used frequently in the criminal justice system, both as a punishment for certain offenses and as a punishment device within the prison or jail. As American society evolved and modernized, corporal punishment fell into disfavor as a punishment for law violators. Many states outlawed the practice. Prisons were somewhat slower to do away with corporal punishment as a means of inmate control. Several southern states permitted the whipping of inmates well into the twentieth century. Arkansas allowed inmates to be whipped until 1965. Corporal punishment has fallen out of favor in corrections, however, and correctional administrators acknowledge that the practice is inappropriate.

Use of Force Generally

Corrections personnel lawfully may use force against inmates in one of five situations (Palmer, 1997). These include:

- In self-defense

- In defense of others

- For enforcement of prison rules and regulations

- To prevent criminal activity within the prison

- To prevent escape

1. Self-defense

Principles of self-defense permit individuals who reasonably fear for their safety to use force to protect themselves from assault. This is true in society generally; it is also true for correctional officers. Correctional officers may use the amount of force necessary to repel an attack and subdue an inmate. Correctional officers may not use any amount of force they deem proper. Rather, they must use only so much force as is necessary under the circumstances to protect themselves. Furthermore, once an officer no longer fears for his or her safety, that officer no longer may be justified in using force against the subdued inmate.

Obviously it is difficult to determine in the heat of the moment how much is "just enough" force. Consequently, courts provide correctional officers with some degree of flexibility, and will not substitute their judgment of reasonableness unless the use of force is clearly greater than that which is necessary, or appears to have been, in the words of the Supreme Court, "malicious and sadistic." While the Eighth Amendment prohibits cruel and unusual punishment, this does not mean that anytime an inmate is injured by correctional personnel that a constitutional violation has occurred. Instead, there must be evidence that the injury occurred when the correctional officer used more force than was reasonable under the circumstances of the case. This is a factual determination; thus, each case is different and must be considered separately.

2. Defense of Others

Correctional officers also may use whatever force is reasonable in defense of others, including fellow officers, other inmates, and visitors. Essentially, the correctional officer may use the same degree of force as the third party (the one being attacked or threatened) could use. This is similar to the general free world rules of self-defense and defense of others.

3. Enforcement of Prison Rules and Discipline

Without rules and regulations, maintaining control of an inmate population would be impossible. And if correctional officers were unable to force recalcitrant inmates to obey these rules and regulations, it, likewise, would be impossible to maintain order in the prison. Thus, courts consistently have recognized that correctional officers may use force to insure inmates comply with institutional rules. Of course, this force must be reasonable under the circumstances.

A number of departments authorize the use of force to prevent inmates from harming themselves, including attemping suicide. While it may seem strange to permit a correctional officer to use force to stop inmates from hurting themselves, there is a distinction between use of

---

force and harm. Correctional officers may use force to prevent what would be a greater harm, even if the inmate is to some degree injured by the use of force.

Other departments authorize the use of force to prevent destruction of property, a common inmate activity. An example is the Federal Bureau of Prisons' policy, which justifies the use of reasonable force to prevent the "serious" destruction of property. The amount of force that would be reasonable to prevent property damage is clearly much less than that permitted to protect a person. This is similar to the free world rules regarding self-defense and defense of property. In most states, persons are justified in using deadly force to save themselves from serious injury, but they never are justified in using deadly force to prevent property damage.

4. Prevention of Criminal Activity

Correctional personnel have a duty to the inmates they supervise to prevent them from foreseeable harm. Failure to do so may constitute "deliberate indifference" and subject the officer to liability under federal statute (42 U.S.C. 1983) and state tort law. This duty to prevent harm includes preventing criminal activity within the prison. This criminal activity may take the form of direct harm to an inmate (as in an assault), or it may take the form of an indirect harm to an inmate (as in criminal activity, such as drug sales or extortion).

Correctional officers are justified in using reasonable force to prevent criminal activity and to apprehend those who commit crimes within prison. They may do so as a means of exercising their duty to protect inmates from harm.

5. Prevention of Escape

In 1997, there were 8,496 reported escapes or escape attempts from correctional facilities. One inmate was killed attempting to escape (Camp, 1998). Correctional officers are permitted to use force to prevent escape, or to recapture an inmate who has escaped. Deadly force may be permitted, depending on the circumstances. While the Supreme Court in *Tennessee v. Garner* (1985) limited police use of deadly force to instances involving the apprehension of a dangerous felon, the high court has never issued a ruling on the appropriate degree of force permitted to prevent inmate escape.

A number of lower courts permit the use of deadly force to prevent the escape of any inmate, on the ground that attempting to escape often is classified as a felony, and under the common law's fleeing felon rule, deadly force could be used to apprehend any fleeing felon, regardless of the severity of the felony (Palmer, 1997). It was the fleeing felon rule that the Supreme Court held unconstitutional in the context of police seizures in *Garner*, however, so this rationale may be suspect.

A number of lower courts still permit the use of deadly force to prevent escape, regardless of the status of the inmate. Lower courts have followed the standard for the use of excessive force established in *Whitley v. Albers* (see page 30), and held that correctional officers may shoot escaping inmates so long as their goal is to prevent escape, and not to "sadistically" cause harm.

A few states allow correctional officers to use deadly force not only to protect themselves or others or prevent escape, but as a means of regaining order. Until recently, California permitted correctional officers to use deadly force (in the form of guns) to stop an inmate-on-inmate fight. As of April 1, 1999, California correctional officers are no longer permitted to use deadly force in such instances, however. This change in policy was a result of a 2.3 million dollar damage award in a case involving an inmate who was shot and killed by a correctional officer attempting to break up a fight (*Corrections Journal*, 1998; *The Corrections Professional*, 1999).

What is "Reasonable" Force?

The general rule for use of force in corrections is that a correctional officer may use such force as is necessary under the circumstances. Reasonable force is the amount of force that is necessary to regain control of the situation, and no more than that. This means that every use of force is judged on the particular facts of the case—no two uses of force are the same, just as no two inmates (or correctional officers) are alike. Clearly, then, to say force must be reasonable hardly ends the inquiry.

Courts look to a number of factors in determining whether the use of force in a specific instance was appropriate. These factors include the amount and type of force used by the inmate and the amount and type of force used by the correctional officer and the perception of the correctional officer. If a reasonable person in the correctional officer's position would have used the same degree of force, then the officer's use of force is appropriate. This test combines subjective and objective components. The subjective components are the consideration of the officer's own point of view. The objective components include the use of the "reasonable person" standard. Under this standard, the court (or jury) must agree that the amount of force used was appropriate and no more than required to regain control.

Standard of Review in Use of Force Cases

Prior to the 1960s, courts rarely even considered use-of-force claims by inmates. But as the hands-off doctrine fell out of favor and courts became more receptive to inmate lawsuits, inmates made an increasing number of claims of excessive force. Courts generally examined these claims under the Eighth Amendment, and the prohibition on "cruel and unusual" punishment. Inmates alleging they had been subject to excessive use of force by correctional staff argued that such force constituted inappropriate punishment. This standard proved difficult to define. Other courts examined excessive force claims under substantive due process and the "shocks the conscience" test (Palmer, 1997). In these cases, courts determined force was excessive only if its application literally shocked the conscience of the judges.

In *Whitley v. Albers* (1986), the Supreme Court expressly held that when an inmate claims correctional personnel have used excessive force, he is raising an Eighth Amendment claim. The Court declined to use the "deliberate indifference" standard, which the court had applied in other Eighth Amendment cases alleging unconstitutional conditions of confinement. Instead, the high court determined that in cases involving allegations of excessive force by corrections staff, the proper standard is as follows:

> whether the measure taken inflicted unnecessary and wanton pain and suffering ultimately turns on whether force was applied in a good faith effort to maintain or restore discipline or maliciously and sadistically for the very purpose of causing harm.

What this means in practical terms is that if force is applied in "a good faith effort to maintain or restore discipline" then no constitutional violation occurs. If, on the other hand, force is applied in a manner, which the court feels indicates a "malicious" or "sadistic" mind set on the part of the correctional officer, then there has been a violation of the constitutional ban on cruel and unusual punishment.

In *Whitley* the inmate plaintiff was shot and seriously injured by a specially trained correctional officer during a prison riot. In its decision, the Court refused to use hindsight to second guess the actions of specially trained corrections personnel. It was unclear whether this subjective standard, focusing on the mind set of the officer, was the appropriate standard for review of all claims of excessive force, including instances where the injury was relatively minor.

In *Hudson v. McMillan* (1992), the Supreme Court declined to limit the standard set forth in *Whitley* to riot situations, and instead extended the standard to cover all use-of-force situations. *Hudson* was a case involving only minor injuries to an inmate. The court went a step beyond the finding in *Whitley* and held that a "significant injury" to an inmate was not necessary for a use of force by correctional personnel to constitute "cruel and unusual punishment."

In this case, a Louisiana inmate being transferred to a different cellblock was punched and kicked by the officer moving him. He did not physically resist; in fact, he was handcuffed and shackled at the time of the beating. The inmate suffered bruises, facial swelling, loosened teeth, and a cracked dental plate. The trial court awarded the inmate some $800 in damages; the court of appeals set aside the verdict and declared that the Eighth Amendment applied only to "significant" injuries.

The Supreme Court reversed the court of appeals, holding that the severity of an inmate's injuries is largely irrelevant in Eighth Amendment claims. In doing so, the court made clear that that the test included both an objective and subjective component: the force must be "reasonable" (objective) and not "malicious or sadistic" (subjective).

The Court also made clear that the extent of the inmate's injuries is just one factor in the inquiry. Just because injuries are "minor" does not mean the use of force was not cruel and unusual punishment. There must be some degree of injury, however—not every use of force amounts to a potential constitutional violation. In the words of the Court, not "every malevolent touch by a guard gives rise to a federal cause of action." The issue in such cases is whether the inmate has suffered "unnecessary and wanton pain," as described in *Whitley*.

The obvious question at this point is, if an injury must be more than a shove, but not serious, how is a correctional officer to know when a violation, in fact, has occurred? The Court declared that the Eighth Amendment "excludes from constitutional recognition de minimis uses of physical force, provided that such use of force is not repugnant to the conscience of mankind." This is still a not altogether clear standard, but it suggests even de minimis (meaning "minor" or "minimal") use of force may be a violation if it is "repugnant" and that generally there must be at least some injury. Unlike a battery, which is complete when someone is touched, some actual injury must occur.

The Supreme Court provided some guidance to correctional staff and administrators when it set forth in *Hudson* the five factors it considered relevant in determining whether correctional personnel have used excessive force in violation of the Constitution (Collins, 1997):

1. Was there a need to use any force?

2. What was the amount of force used?

3. What injuries, if any, were inflicted?

4. What was the threat perceived by responsible correctional officials?

5. What efforts to temper the use of force were made?

Correctional administrators can use these factors as a starting point for evaluating use-of-force incidents.

Use of Deadly Force

Thus, correctional personnel are justified in using "reasonable" force to maintain security. A question, which often arises, during prison riots or escape attempts, is whether deadly force is permitted. While the Supreme Court has not ruled directly on the use of deadly force in corrections, it has provided guidelines on the use of deadly force for police officers. In *Tennessee v. Garner* (1985), the Supreme Court ruled that police may not shoot a fleeing suspect, unless the officer reasonably feared for his or her safety, or the safety of others.

It is unlikely that the Supreme Court would hold correctional officers to the same standard as that of police officers, given the different circumstances. A fleeing (or escaping) inmate is different from a mere suspect, who has not been convicted of a crime. Lower courts consistently have upheld the use of deadly force to prevent escape from correctional facilities (Walker, 1996). Justification for the use of deadly force include the fact that escapees, by virtue of their conviction, have proven themselves willing to break the law, and thus are more clearly a danger to the public than a mere suspect in a case, as was the situation in *Garner*. Walker's (1996) review of lower court cases dealing with the use of deadly force by corrections personnel reveals courts generally see prison escapees as a much greater threat to society than criminal suspects.

Less than Lethal Force

Correctional officers, in most instances, will not be called on to use deadly force. A much more frequent occurrence is the use of nondeadly force. Nondeadly force is routinely used for mundane purposes, such as to remove reluctant inmates from their cells. So long as the amount of force used is "reasonable" under the circumstances, the use of force is likely to be considered appropriate.

The advent of new technology has made possible the use of nondeadly force in situations where a correctional officer previously may have used deadly force. A less-than-lethal force weapon is much less likely to result in death when used (Miller, 1995). Examples of less-than-lethal force weapons include batons, plastic bullets, chemical weapons (such as Mace), and electronic stun devices (such as Tasers).

Correctional Officer Liability

An area of the law of great concern to correctional personnel is the issue of liability. It is important to distinguish the different duties owed by correctional personnel. The correctional officer, as a quasi law-enforcement agent, owes a duty to the public to protect it from harm. There is an obligation to keep inmates deemed dangerous away from the public. This duty includes keeping such individuals in secure custody to prevent escape, and to keep such inmates incarcerated until it is determined that they pose no future danger to society.

Correctional officers also owe a duty to the inmates they supervise. Corrections personnel may not knowingly harm an inmate unless the harm occurs as part of a legitimate use of force, nor may staff manifest "deliberate indifference" to the safety, security, and health of an inmate.

Legal Remedies for Harm

There are several bases for correctional personnel liability. The most common are state tort law, the Federal Tort Claims Act of 1946, and the Federal Civil Rights Act of 1871 (42 U.S.C. Section 1983). The Federal Tort Claims Act of 1946 waives the sovereign immunity of the federal government in a number of areas, and 42 U.S.C. Section 1983 provides a federal law remedy for injury caused by state agents.

Section 1983 Actions

The vast majority of inmate lawsuits involving the actions of correctional personnel are brought under 42 U.S.C. 1983. This federal statute, also referred to as the Civil Rights Act, originally was intended to provide a means of redress for freed slaves injured by southern state officials. While Section 1983 was passed by Congress in 1871, it was not until *Monroe v. Pape,* (1961) that the Supreme Court held that the law applied to the violation of civil rights of criminal suspects. The U.S. Supreme Court has determined that the law as written also applied to the corrections setting. Section 1983 states:

> Every person who, under color of any statute, ordinance, regulation, custom, or usage, of any state or territory, subjects, or causes to be subject, any citizen of the United States or other person within the jurisdiction thereof to the deprivation of any rights, privileges, or immunities secured by the Constitution and laws, shall be liable to the party injured in an action at law, suit in equity, or other proper proceeding for damages.

To succeed under a Section 1983 claim, the plaintiff must establish several points:

(1) There was an injury to the plaintiff.

(2) This injury involved a violation of a constitutional right or a federal law.

(3) The defendant was a person. The Supreme Court has determined that Section 1983 actions may not be brought against the state or a state agency, as these are not considered persons. However, the Supreme Court has permitted local municipalities to be sued under Section 1983. Thus, cities and counties may be sued under Section 1983 for injuries that occur in their jails.

(4) The defendant was acting "under color of law." This means that the injury was a result of misconduct by a state agent acting in his or her role as a state agent.

(5) The defendant must be involved in the injury, either by committing it himself or herself or by causing it to occur, either through a failure to properly supervise a subordinate when he or she was aware the subordinate was violating the law (in other words, deliberate indifference); or by failing to train when there was an obvious need to do so (again, deliberate indifference).

There are two forms of relief available to prevailing plaintiffs under Section 1983. They may seek an injunction, whereby the court orders the defendant to stop committing the constitutional violation. Plaintiffs also may seek money damages from the defendant. This has clear implications for correctional personnel!

State Tort Law

State tort law varies a great deal from state to state; consequently, correctional personnel are advised to familiarize themselves with the law in their jurisdiction. Several principles generally apply, however.

A tort is a civil wrong. There are three conditions which must exist for a tort to be proven. First, it must be shown that the defendant owed a duty to the plaintiff. This duty may arise from law, as in the case of contracts, or from the relationship of the plaintiff and defendant.

Second, it also must be shown that the defendant not only owed a duty to the plaintiff, but that he or she breached that duty. In legal parlance, there are three forms that this breach of duty may take in regards to state agents. If a person takes an improper action, it is termed *misfeasance*. If the individual takes no action or takes a required action but performs it inappropriately, it is termed *malfeasance*.

The third condition for a tort is a demonstration that the injury suffered by the plaintiff was, in fact, the proximate consequence of the defendant's breach of duty. Proximate cause is a legal creation intended to limit liability for damages to consequences that are reasonably foreseeable and related to the defendant's conduct.

A prevailing plaintiff in a state tort action may seek either an injunction or money damages. Additionally, under the common law doctrine of respondeat superior, a supervisor may be liable for the actions of his or her subordinates.

Immunity

At common law, the state could not be sued for civil damages as a result of its actions, regardless of the intent of the state. Under the English doctrine of sovereign immunity, the king, as an agent of God, was considered incapable of doing wrong; hence, there was no possibility of liability. This doctrine has continued, in watered-down fashion, to the present day.

Most states have some statutory provision waiving their sovereign immunity in certain circumstances. This allows lawsuits to be brought in state court relying on state tort law. A tort is a "private or civil wrong or injury other than beach of contract, for which the court will provide a remedy in the form of an action for damages" (Black, 1983).

While the federal and state governments provide for a waiver of their sovereign immunity in some circumstances, this waiver is far from complete. There are three forms of immunity defenses invoked in liability suits: absolute, qualified, and quasijudicial immunity (Jones and del Carmen, 1992). Under absolute immunity, a lawsuit is dismissed without delving into the merits of the claim itself. Qualified immunity protects an official only if the official acted in "good faith," meaning he or she violated rights which were not clearly established in law. Under quasijudicial immunity, official duties that are nondiscretionary are not protected from liability, while official duties that involve the exercise of discretion are accorded protection from liability.

Summary

This chapter examines an area, which many correctional officers and administrators would like to avoid entirely. The day has not yet come that a correctional officer needs to think like a lawyer, however. If correctional officers can remember a few main points, they should be able to do their jobs effectively without infringing on the constitutional rights of the inmates they supervise or incurring liability.

When there is an incident involving a use of force by correctional personnel, they should remember to follow institutional policy, attempt to settle the situation by the least force necessary, and be sure to document their actions. Proper documentation is time consuming, but essential. Documentation is discussed in greater detail in Chapter 4.

Criminal justice offenders do not enjoy the same rights as ordinary citizens. But where rights have been circumscribed, certain procedures still must be followed. This is the essence of the phrase "due process of law." And while correctional officers need not be lawyers, it would be wise for them to keep abreast of the latest developments in the area.

Use-of-Force Policies, Practices, and Procedures: Results of a National Survey

Jeff Maahs

Travis Pratt

Craig Hemmens

Introduction

Even though the use of force in corrections is an important issue for criminal justice policymakers, correctional administrators, and correctional staff, there has been relatively little research on the topic. This chapter presents a summary of the results of a survey sent to the administrators of correctional agencies in the United States and the Canadian provinces. The survey focused on various aspects of the use of force, including use-of-force policy provisions, use-of-force training, and use-of-force incident reporting. The survey was sent to state and federal prisons, a sample of major jails, and state juvenile facilities. The survey was sponsored by the American Correctional Association and administered by Dr. Hemmens.

The results of this survey are useful for several reasons. First, this represents the most comprehensive survey of use-of-force policies ever conducted. For the first time, correctional administrators can get an idea of what other departments are doing and see what sorts of issues and concerns other departments have.

Second, the research findings provide correctional administrators with the "big picture" regarding current use-of-force policies—administrators can compare their department's policies with national trends. This is useful in pointing out areas where policies and procedures may be lagging behind other departments, or where there are important issues that are not addressed by their use-of-force policies and procedures.

Third, the research findings provide those outside of corrections with an idea of what corrections departments are doing to monitor, evaluate, and control the use of force by correctional officers. The quantity and specificity of correctional use-of-force policies revealed in this research will demonstrate to those not familiar with correctional practice just how proactive corrections departments have become in maintaining the appropriate level of force.

Survey Administration

The survey instrument was developed by Dr. Hemmens, in consultation with the American Correctional Association and several experts in correctional use of force. The questionnaire included questions about: (1) the existence of use-of-force policies, (2) the content of these policies, (3) the process by which the department monitors use of force incidents, (4) the amount and type of training on use of force provided to correctional officers, and (5) the type and number of use-of-force incidents reported during the past year. Copies of the department use-of-force policy and any related materials and forms (such as training manuals and prepared report forms) also were requested.

The questionnaire was distributed by mail to the corrections departments of all fifty states, the Federal Bureau of Prisons, U.S. military organizations, and the Canadian provinces. Surveys also were mailed to the juvenile corrections/juvenile welfare agency in each state. Additionally, surveys were mailed to a sample of ninety of the largest American jails.

Mailing lists were provided by the American Correctional Association, which also oversaw the mail distribution of the surveys.

The survey was sent out in late 1997. After a number of surveys were completed and returned, a second mailing of the survey was conducted in early 1998. Those departments that had not responded to the two mailings were contacted by phone and asked to participate. In the end, a total of 170 surveys were returned. Forty-six of the fifty state departments of corrections responded, for a response rate of 92 percent. The Federal Bureau of Prisons and two military corrections departments also responded. Eight of the thirteen Canadian corrections departments responded to the survey. Eight states have a combined juvenile and adult system; of the remaining forty-two states, thirty-nine state juvenile agencies responded, for a response rate of 93 percent. Only thirty of the ninety jails (33 percent) responded. This is a relatively low response rate, but not surprising, given the lack of a specialized research staff in most large jails.

The 170 returned surveys were entered into a software statistical package (SPSS), and the data was analyzed using a variety of statistical procedures. The results of this data analysis are presented, in both text and table format, for ease of presentation and comprehension. A copy of the survey is located in Appendix C.

Findings

The various areas of the survey are discussed in the sections below. The responses of the state departments of correction, juvenile justice agencies, and jails are presented separately in the tables for analysis and comparison. The focus of the discussion, however, is on the results obtained from the state departments of correction.

Excluded from the analysis are the responses of the Federal Bureau of Prisons and the two military organizations, which responded, to maintain anonymity. However, the responses of these three departments were in large part very similar to the responses of state corrections departments.

Use of Force Definition

The first survey question asked whether the department or facility had a written use-of-force policy. Almost every institution has a written use-of-force policy. All of the forty-six state agencies that responded to the survey indicated that they have a written use-of-force policy. Additionally, 97 percent of the juvenile agencies and 97 percent of the jails also have a written use-of-force policy. This is not surprising, as corrections departments at all levels have become much more bureaucratized and professional standards have been widely adopted.

While all state corrections departments have a written use-of-force policy, individual departments define the use of force in a variety of ways. One survey item asked the departments to provide their use-of-force policy definition. Most of the definitions focus on describing what constitutes force. Examples include: "physical contact or threats of physical contact with an inmate to control behavior or to enforce order," "physical contact deliberately made with an inmate in a confrontational situation to control the inmate," and "any force used against an offender other than incidental contact, including physical handling, firearms, and chemical agents."

Other definitions include not only what constitutes force, but what constitutes an acceptable amount of force or when force is appropriate. Examples include: "that degree of force necessary to control the situation," and "that force that is reasonably necessary to perform duties and protect from harm."

There are some common definitions of the use of force. At the same time, there is some variation in the specificity of the definition. Several departments have very short, general definitions; other departments have much more detailed definitions, including, in some cases, a complete continuum of the amount of force appropriate in different situations.

Use of Force Policy

A number of questions in the survey were directed at the specifics of department use-of-force policies. Questions included whether a department has a written use-of-force policy, whether the use-of-force policy has provisions dealing with special situations (such as restraint techniques and specialized confinement areas), and whether the policy addresses how to deal with the escalation of force. Table 4.1 displays information dealing with written use-of-force policies.

TABLE 4.1
CONTENT OF USE OF FORCE POLICIES BY PERCENTAGE

Agency	Have a written policy	Specialized applications of force	Specialized restraint techniques	Special confinement conditions	Policy for escalation of force
U.S. DOCs	100	83	45	55	92
Canada DOCs	100	57	57	86	100
Jails	97	83	53	41	97
Juvenile	97	70	64	56	73

Specialized Applications of Force

An overwhelming majority (83 percent) of state corrections departments have policies dealing with specialized applications of force, such as four-point restraints. Interestingly, the Canadian institutions are much less likely (only 57 percent) to have specific policies regarding this issue.

Specialized Restraint Techniques

While most state corrections departments have written policies dealing with specialized applications of force, less than half (45 percent) have policies dealing with specialized restraint techniques. Jails are also much less likely to have such policies than they are to have policies dealing with specialized applications of force.

This is an area of some concern, given the increased proliferation of less-than-lethal weapons technology, which allows correctional officers a fuller range of responses. New devices are being introduced to corrections at a rapid rate. It is unclear from court opinions, for example, where the use of chemical agents falls on the use-of-force continuum. Should a correctional officer resort to pepper spray before engaging in physical contact or will this be interpreted as an overreaction? Courts only now are beginning to address this issue.

Corrections departments need to be proactive and take the lead in developing clear guidelines for the new use-of-force techniques and technologies, rather than waiting for the courts to enter the fray. If corrections departments provide adequate training and supervision in use-of-force techniques and technologies, and are able to provide defensible approaches to uses of force, then courts are more likely to defer to the practices of corrections departments rather than instituting their own standards.

Specialized Confinement Conditions

All dangerous, high-risk inmates are managed throughout the country with additional options, such as strip cells or removal to time out spaces. These confinement options are intended to manage the inmate who has become so continuously disruptive that he or she is having a seriously negative impact on the remainder of the living area. Usually these are the inmates who engaged in loud hollering, screaming, door banging, flooding of their cell, and where possible, destruction of cell property.

In cases where the inmate is not eligible for, nor will voluntarily accept, a sedative medication, and is unresponsive to attempts at constructive dialog, it becomes necessary to use some of these options available to change his or her behavior. The inmate may have his or her existing cell cleared of all personal property and be required to change out of prison uniform and into light clothing in the form of personal underwear or a jumpsuit. All normal privileges may be temporarily suspended (exercise, shower, property, and so forth). The inmate is then left in the cell with a pillow and, where temperatures require, a light blanket.

An additional alternative would be to move the inmate to a time-out cell away from the main living unit. In such cases, the inmate would remain under frequent supervisory checks. The effect is to eliminate the possibility of self-harming acts and deliver a strong message to the inmate that it is time to begin to control his or her behavior appropriately. As behavior improves, property may be returned to the extent that the inmate returns to normal conditions. Often in this process of inmate movement or removal of property from the cell, inmate behavior may prompt the need to use force. This kind of activity is often controversial. It is important for the effective management of high-risk offenders, and it should be expressed in policy, procedure, and specialized training.

As the survey indicates, many state departments of corrections are also without written policies governing the use of specialized confinement conditions, such as strip cells. Only slightly over half (55 percent) of state departments of corrections address this issue. Canadian institutions, on the other hand, are much more likely (86 percent) to have a policy addressing this issue.

When is Escalation Okay?

Virtually all state corrections departments (92 percent) and even more jails that responded to the survey (97 percent) provide guidance as to when escalation in the amount of force involved in a use-of-force incident may be appropriate. This is in accord with guidelines in other areas, including law enforcement, where it is essential that officers be provided with clear and specific guidelines on selecting the type and amount of force and when it is appropriate to consider other force options based on a difference in circumstances.

Use of Force Equipment

As Table 4.1 indicates, many departments' use-of-force policies include a discussion of specialized use-of-force equipment. Departments also were asked what particular types of use-of-force equipment are authorized for use by correctional officers involved in a use-of-force incident. Table 4.2 indicates that most agencies now use a wide range of equipment to subdue inmates.

TABLE 4.2

PERCENTAGE OF INSTITUTIONS WITH SELECTED USE OF FORCE EQUIPMENT

Agency	Chemical Agents	Stun Guns	Shields	Firearms	Body Armor	Videotape Equipment	Other
U.S. DOCs	98	43	95	93	88	87	55
Canada DOCs	100	0	83	17	50	57	33
Jails	77	37	87	77	90	59	70
Juvenile	30	3	32	11	22	22	73

The majority of state correctional agencies reported using chemical agents, stun guns, shields, and body armor as "nonlethal" alternatives to firearms. Chemical agents were the most frequently mentioned less-than-lethal weapon, used by 98 percent of state corrections departments. Shields (95 percent) and firearms (93 percent) also are used by virtually every state corrections department.

Most state corrections departments (87 percent) now videotape use-of-force incidents. Videotape serves the purpose of documenting the incident, to be used as a defense to inmate claims of excessive force. It also provides the department with more information than a written report, thus allowing for more thorough departmental review of incidents. Video may serve not only to provide better documentation of what happens, but also to provide a check on improper activity of staff, who may be deterred from inappropriate conduct when they are aware that their actions are being recorded for review by supervisors. Video recordings also may be used as evidence in defense of claims of excessive force, and as a tool to educate in a court of law. Judges tend to pay careful attention when they can view documented evidence that staff are professional and effective in the face of inmate conduct that is highly disruptive.

Corrections departments should be wary of how videotape will play out in the public eye, however; what appears reasonable to a seasoned correctional officer familiar with a particular inmate may appear excessive to the public.

Special Response Team

Corrections work has become increasingly specialized. This increase in specialization also has occurred in use-of-force situations. Many departments now have specialized response teams, as Table 4.3 indicates.

Table 4.3 reveals that most state corrections departments (87 percent) have developed special teams to handle use-of-force incidents. Interestingly, jails lag slightly behind in this area, perhaps because of the additional expense and training that is required for such units.

Only 17 percent of juvenile agencies have developed specialized response teams. This is not surprising, given that most juvenile detention facilities still have as their primary purpose the protection of the child, and the recognition that children, even those who have offended, must be

Table 4.3

Use of Special Response Team in Percentage

Agency	Special team for use-of-force incidents
U.S. DOCs	87
Canada DOCs	86
Jails	76
Juvenile	17

treated differently than adults. When looked at in this light, the fact that any juvenile detention facility has developed specialized response teams indicates that there has been a shift either in the type of juveniles committed or the philosophy of juvenile corrections, or both.

Specialized use-of-force teams should have the advantage of being trained for the situation, so that they are better prepared to handle potential disturbances; additionally, their presence may serve to deter inmate misconduct: an inmate may refuse to leave his or her cell for a regular officer, but when the extraction team is called and appears in body armor at the door, recalcitrant inmates may well change their minds and exit without physical violence. This assumes that these response teams, in fact, receive additional training and are not simply a collection of volunteers. Unfortunately, it is unknown at this point whether the response teams are better trained.

Administrative Review of Use of Force Incidents

As the discussion of legal liability and judicial oversight of corrections practice in Chapter 3 made clear, review of use-of-force incidents is a vital piece of the puzzle. Review of use-of-force incidents provides the department with information about what happened, how future incidents can be prevented or minimized, and provides the basis for defending inmate claims of excessive use of force.

The Review Process

When an incident requiring use of force takes place, most correctional institutions follow procedural guidelines to document the incident in case there is a dispute over whether the use of force was proper. Table 4.4 displays information pertaining to the type and extent of the review process.

The survey included a number of questions concerning the review process for use-of-force incidents. Areas examined included the incident report, the steps in the review process, and who is involved in the review process.

Written Report

All of the respondents indicated that a written report is required for all use-of-force incidents. This is true for every state corrections department, Canadian institution, jail, and juvenile facility. This, perhaps more clearly than anything else, reveals the degree to which corrections work has become increasingly bureaucratized. Operations have become standardized, and more formal procedures have replaced informal means of dealing with situations. While this means more paperwork, it also means an increase in accountability and professionalization. These are clearly positive outcomes, for both the inmate and the correctional officer. While writing up a report may be an unpleasant chore, it is also a means of documenting an event and providing the officer with the information necessary to defend against any claims of excessive force.

TABLE 4.4

ADMINISTRATIVE OVERSIGHT OF USE-OF-FORCE INCIDENTS IN PERCENTAGE

Agency	Written Report	Prepared Form	Administrative Review Process	All Incidents Subject to Review	Report to Central Authority	Formal, Written Statement Required	Interview
U.S. DOCs	100	95	97	95	90	59	53
Canada DOCs	100	67	100	86	86	43	57
Jails	100	87	93	97	93	79	48
Juvenile	100	100	95	89	76	54	66

Prepared Form

The vast majority (95 percent) of state corrections departments go one step beyond requiring a written report and provide a prepared form to be completed by the involved correctional officer. This facilitates the reporting process, increases uniformity of information collected, and consequently protects the officer and department from liability by providing a clearer picture of the incident for use in a trial years later.

Interestingly, while virtually all corrections departments require a written report, only 59 percent require the officer(s) involved to complete a formal written statement in their own words describing what occurred. It appears that many departments instead rely simply on a prepared, fill-in-the-blank type of form.

Administrative Review Process

Almost all of the agencies have an administrative review process, and most report that all use-of-force incidents are subject to review. There is less consensus, however, among the agencies concerning the involvement of a central authority in the review process (see Table 4.5). Although a high percentage of state departments of correction (68 percent) do require a central administrative structure in their review process, juvenile agencies (59 percent), Canadian corrections agencies (43 percent), and jails (23 percent) are far less formalized in reviewing use-of-force incidents.

As Table 4.4 also indicates, virtually all incidents involving use of force are subject to review by state corrections departments. While review is a virtual guarantee, the form of the review differs among the departments. Only 59 percent of state corrections departments require a formal, written statement, and only 53 percent require an interview with the officer(s) involved. While the number of departments, which require either a written statement or an interview is substantially lower than the other requirements, examination of the responses indicated no discernible pattern among corrections departments. That is, departments of different sizes and in different geographical regions of the country were no more or less likely to require formal written statements or interviews.

TABLE 4.5

ADMINISTRATIVE LEVELS PARTICIPATING IN THE REVIEW PROCESS BY PERCENTAGE

Agency	Shift Leader	Manager	Super-intendent	Regional Staff	Central Office Staff	Other
U.S. DOCs	77	59	73	39	68	25
Canada DOCs	71	71	86	57	43	29
Jails	93	53	40	7	23	53
Juvenile	79	85	80	21	59	21

Who Conducts the Review?

Respondents also were asked about who participates in the review process concerning use-of-force incidents. Table 4.5 indicates a number of different levels in the corrections department typically are involved.

Not surprisingly, the individual most often involved in the review process is the person closest to the situation, the shift leader. Others frequently involved in the review process are the superintendent/warden, and central office staff. These responses indicate that in many departments, the review process includes virtually every administrative level.

Policy Review Method

Another area of concern is proactive in approach rather than reactive (unlike review of incidents). Respondents were asked how frequently the use-of-force policy is reviewed and/or updated by administrators, and how often the use-of-force policy is reviewed with line staff. This is particularly important, as new technology and court decisions can change what is permitted and possible very quickly.

If an agency has a quality policy review process, it normally would include a formal, annual review process. In this process, subject matter experts would insure that each policy, including use of force, would be updated with changes presented for approval to the executive staff. Table 4.6 reveals that most agencies also have a fairly informal method of updating and/or reviewing their use-of-force policies. While many do so

TABLE 4.6

UPDATE AND/OR REVIEW OF USE-OF-FORCE POLICIES IN PERCENTAGE

Agency	Never	Daily	Annual Training	Special Session	Major Incident	Don't Know	Other
U.S. DOCs	0	5	54	13	26	3	41
Canada DOCs	0	0	29	14	57	14	43
Jails	0	0	59	21	17	10	45
Juvenile	5	5	65	16	19	8	38

during annual training sessions, a significant portion of agencies do so only after a major incident has occurred. This suggests the review and revision process is still reactive in many departments, rather than serving to prevent possible problems.

A significant portion of corrections departments indicated "other" when asked when they review their use-of-force policies. Unfortunately, most did not explain this response. It is possible that many departments checked the "other" response to indicate they review their use-of-force policies at several different times, rather than just at one fixed time.

Frequency of Policy Review

The frequency that use-of-force policies are reviewed with line officers follows a similar trend. As seen in Table 4.7, aside from annual training sessions, many agencies review their use-of-force policies with officers in the absence of a formal procedure. The most common time for policy review is during annual training. Another not surprising fact is that many departments review their use-of-force policies after a major incident has occurred. This accords with when corrections departments review their policies and procedures.

Training on Use of Force

A key component in the effort to avoid the occurrence of excessive or inappropriate use of force is training. Respondents were asked several

TABLE 4.7

REVIEW OF USE-OF-FORCE POLICIES WITH LINE OFFICERS IN PERCENTAGE

Agency	Never	Daily	Annual Training	Special Session	Major Incident	Don't Know	Other
U.S. DOCs	3	3	80	18	13	5	36
Canada DOCs	0	0	43	29	57	0	14
Jails	0	0	72	31	31	3	38
Juvenile	0	3	87	24	26	0	29

questions concerning the amount and type of training provided relating to use-of-force incidents. This included training on use-of-force techniques and equipment, self-defense training, and the policy on use of force. They also were asked about crisis intervention and dealing with difficult/aggressive inmates.

Across all agencies surveyed, the training involved in the different aspects of the use of force is extensive. Table 4.8 indicates that correctional officers, in nearly all cases, are given formal training on the equipment, techniques, and philosophy regarding the use of force in their respective agencies.

TABLE 4.8

FORMAL TRAINING FOR DIFFERENT ASPECTS OF USE-OF-FORCE IN PERCENTAGE

Agency	Equipment	Techniques	Philosophy
U.S. DOCs	98	98	95
Canada DOCs	100	100	100
Jails	100	97	97
Juvenile	100	97	97

TABLE 4.9

NUMBER OF REQUIRED HOURS OF SELF-DEFENSE TRAINING IN PERCENTAGE*

Agency	0 hours	1-10 hours	11-20 hours	21-30 hours	31-40 hours	41+ hours
U.S. DOCs	0	38	20	23	8	12
Canada DOCs	0	0	80	20	0	0
Jails	0	13	27	10	17	33
Juvenile	18	18	39	8	5	13

* Numbers may not add to 100 percent due to rounding.

Although the number of hours spent in training varies considerably (*see* Table 4.9), officers are provided with a wide array of training on methods and techniques for self-defense (*see* Table 4.10).

TABLE 4.10

TYPES OF SELF-DEFENSE TRAINING PROVIDED IN PERCENTAGE

Agency	Aikido	Firearms	Restraint Techniques	Chemical Agents	Conflict Resolution	Other
U.S. DOCs	30	95	98	98	78	48
Canada DOCs	33	17	100	100	100	33
Jails	7	90	93	76	86	38
Juvenile	16	11	87	29	84	40

Inmate Assaults

The majority of use-of-force incidents involve a correctional officer responding to an assault by an inmate (Kratcoski, 1987; Light, 1991). This may be characterized as self-defense, or may involve subduing an inmate. Several survey questions dealt with the issue of inmate assaults. Respondents were asked where use-of-force incidents most often occur in the institution, and how often and in what manner correctional officers were attacked by inmates during the past year.

TABLE 4.11

WHERE IN THE INSTITUTION USE-OF-FORCE INCIDENTS MOST OFTEN OCCUR, IN PERCENTAGE

Agency	Housing Area	Work Area	Recreation Area	Eating Area	Hospital Area	Don't Know	Other
U.S. DOCs	88	0	20	5	3	5	25
Canada DOCs	83	17	67	17	17	0	50
Jails	73	3	17	13	3	0	57
Juvenile	90	5	33	13	0	5	18

Location of Use-of-force Incidents

As Table 4.11 indicates, all of the agencies reported that use-of-force incidents tend to occur in either the housing area or the recreation area. This is in accord with prior research on use of force (Kratcoski, 1987; Light, 1991), which is discussed in Chapter 1.

Number of Attacks on Staff

Agencies do, however, vary widely in terms of the number of inmate attacks on staff that occur annually. This is in accord with other research (Camp and Camp, 1998) which reported 14,359 assaults against staff in 1997. Table 4.12 shows that while only a handful of juvenile agencies reported no attacks on staff, the adult corrections departments varied

TABLE 4.12

NUMBER OF INMATE ATTACKS ON STAFF IN 1997, IN PERCENTAGE

Agency	0	1-25	26-50	51-75	76-100	101-125	126-150	151+
U.S. DOCs	0	21	15	6	12	3	6	36
Canada DOCs	0	71	0	14	0	0	0	14
Jails	0	46	19	15	0	4	4	12
Juvenile	6	50	9	6	13	0	0	16

widely in the number of inmate assaults on staff. This is, of course, in large part a function of the size of the department—the larger the department, the more inmates under supervision, and (all else being equal) the greater the number of attacks. A significant number of agencies reported more than 151 attacks.

Number of Attacks with a Weapon

Despite the variability in the number of inmate attacks on staff that occur annually, few of these attacks involved a weapon. Table 4.13 shows that the number of times inmates used a weapon on staff in the last year was, for the most part, twenty-five times or less for any given agency. There was, on the other hand, a small percentage of agencies on the "high end" that experienced more than 151 inmate attacks involving a weapon.

TABLE 4.13

NUMBER OF INMATE ATTACKS WITH A WEAPON ON STAFF IN 1997 IN PERCENTAGE

Agency	0	1-25	26-50	51-75	76-100	101-125	126-150	151+
U.S. DOCs	24	46	9	3	0	0	6	12
Canada DOCs	50	50	0	0	0	0	0	0
Jails	36	55	5	0	0	0	0	5
Juvenile	58	39	3	0	0	0	0	0

Use-of-force Incidents

Similar to the number of inmate attacks on staff, the number of use-of-force incidents that occurred in 1997 also varies widely among correctional agencies. Some agencies reported having between only 1 to 25 incidents, while others reported having more than 151 (see Table 4.14). Again, this is likely a function of the size of the department—the bigger the department, the more inmates; the more inmates, the more use-of-force incidents.

TABLE 4.14

NUMBER OF USE-OF-FORCE INCIDENTS THAT OCCURRED IN 1997 IN PERCENTAGE

Agency	0	1-25	26-50	51-75	76-100	101-125	126-150	151+
U.S. DOCs	0	9	13	3	3	3	0	69
Canada DOCs	0	57	14	0	0	0	0	29
Jails	0	17	9	9	4	0	13	48
Juvenile	0	17	23	0	7	0	7	47

Number of Excessive Force Incidents

Respondents also were asked how many use-of-force incidents in the past year were determined to involve excessive force. Table 4.15 reveals that a significant percentage (40 percent) of corrections departments reported no excessive force incidents, while another 55 percent reported fewer than twenty-five excessive force incidents.

Given the high number of use-of-force incidents in corrections, this suggests that correctional officers are acting appropriately in the vast majority of cases. In other words, for every single excessive use of force in corrections that reaches judicial review and possible media attention, there are hundreds, perhaps thousands, that occur across the country that are performed for the right reasons in a professional manner. This perspective is too often forgotten in the face of isolated events.

TABLE 4.15

NUMBER OF "EXCESSIVE" USE-OF-FORCE INCIDENTS IN PERCENTAGE

Agency	0	1-25	26-50	51-75	76-100	101-125	126-150	151+
U.S. DOCs	40	55	0	0	0	3	0	3
Canada DOCs	60	40	0	0	0	0	0	0
Jails	37	63	0	0	0	0	0	0
Juvenile	36	45	3	13	0	0	0	3

TABLE 4.16

NUMBER OF EXCESSIVE USE-OF-FORCE INCIDENTS THAT RESULTED IN DISCIPLINARY ACTION FOR CORRECTIONAL PERSONNEL IN PERCENTAGE

Agency	0	1-25	26-50	51-75	76-100	101-125	126-150	151+
U.S. DOCs	37	57	0	0	0	0	3	3
Canada DOCs	67	33	0	0	0	0	0	0
Jails	27	73	0	0	0	0	0	0
Juvenile	35	55	3	7	0	0	0	0

Disciplinary Action

Table 4.16 reveals that disciplinary action for excessive force was taken in only a small number of cases. Ninety-four percent of state corrections departments had fewer than twenty-five instances where correctional officers were disciplined for using excessive force. Again, this suggests that excessive force is a relatively infrequent occurrence.

Inmate Lawsuits

As stated earlier, inmate lawsuits are an important issue for correctional agencies. As seen in Table 4.17, most agencies are facing only a small number of inmate lawsuits alleging the unlawful use of force. Indeed, many have no lawsuits pending. However, 30 percent of U.S. departments of corrections currently are dealing with more than fifty-one

TABLE 4.17

NUMBER OF CURRENT INMATE LAWSUITS ALLEGING UNLAWFUL USE OF FORCE IN PERCENTAGE

Agency	0	1-10	11-20	21-30	31-40	41-50	51+	Don't know
U.S. DOCs	13	30	13	3	3	3	30	5
Canada DOCs	67	33	0	0	0	0	0	0
Jails	27	58	7	4	0	0	0	4
Juvenile	81	16	3	0	0	0	0	0

of these inmate lawsuits. Thus, the unlawful use of force (or at least the perception of such on the part of inmates) is still an ongoing problem for correctional administrators.

While a number of departments are facing a substantial number (fifty-one or more) of inmate lawsuits, this figure may be somewhat misleading. The mere fact that a department has a large number of pending lawsuits does not necessarily mean there are problems with use of force in that department. Rather, the high number of lawsuits simply may be a function of the size of the department—the bigger the department, the more inmates it has; the more inmates, the greater the likelihood of confrontation; the more confrontations that occur, the greater the likelihood that an inmate will file a lawsuit alleging excessive use of force. Further research on the ratio of lawsuits to department size is needed.

Staffing Issues

Correctional agencies also were surveyed concerning staffing and security issues. These responses are displayed in Table 4.18. As correctional populations continue to climb, corrections departments are faced with increasing staff to ensure adequate supervision and monitoring of the inmate population. As Table 4.18 indicates, at least 16 percent of corrections departments in the United States and 14 percent in Canada report not having enough staff for adequate security, and even more departments report having to close security posts because of a shortage of staff.

Table 4.18

Security Issues by Percentage

Agency	Enough staff for adequate security	Security posts closed due to staff shortage
U.S. DOCs	84	70
Canada DOCs	86	14
Jails	87	36
Juvenile	75	29

Among juvenile agencies, 25 percent report not having enough staff for adequate security; this is not an insignificant number. Of greater concern, however, is the fact that 70 percent of state corrections departments report having to sometimes close security posts because of staffing shortages. This is a large number and clearly indicates that at times, security may be compromised because of staffing problems.

Special Inmates Issues

Table 4.19 reveals that virtually all state departments of correction provide some form of specialized confinement area for disruptive inmates. These specialized confinement areas vary widely in name and form. As might be expected, juvenile facilities less frequently have such facilities, but surprisingly, almost 74 percent do have some sort of specialized confinement area.

TABLE 4.19
SECURITY ISSUES BY PERCENTAGE

Agency	Special cells for violent or disruptive inmates
U.S. DOCs	95
Canada DOCs	100
Jails	90
Juvenile	74

Summary

This research indicates that corrections departments in the United States in large part have endorsed and implemented policies, procedures, and training regarding the use of force. This research also has revealed, however, that there are significant variations in how use-of-force policies and procedures are implemented. The range of training and the frequency of policy review are but two examples of the variation that exists. While no two department policies are alike, there are a number of similarities. In the appendix are examples of use-of-force policies from three state correctional departments, the Federal Bureau of Prisons' use-of-force policy, and the American Correctional Association Standards relating to use of force.

Current Practices

Current Practices

Quality management of a correctional facility is directly related to staff being trained and committed to being highly effective communicators and problem solvers with inmates. Most often, it is those kinds of skills that diffuse tense situations and avoid conflict. However, under the best of circumstances, staff must intervene forcefully. It is a reality of the profession. The decision to use force is situational, and the competent application of force is one of the most crucial acts correctional officers perform. To view the use of force as being any less important invites the possibility of serious litigation, an extremely negative public view of the profession, strong support for the notion that the agency has failed to achieve its mission, and criticism of the leadership and philosophy of the organization. For use of force to be managed successfully, all critical functions such as training, procedures, oversight, employee attitude, and performance must flow from a thoughtful, precise policy. There is perhaps no single more important document in corrections than a precise policy on the use of force.

The types of force used by correctional agencies in each situation are commonly selected according to their effectiveness in responding to the level and type of resistance offered by inmates. The selection depends on the circumstances related to each incident. The total number of force options allowed by agencies usually are determined by the conditions presented by the inmate population, history of experience with various options, legal decisions, legislation, and departmental policy. Note that the community of correctional professionals, as with many issues, has differing views on use of force and all should not be expected to agree on every aspect.

All levels of force must never be used as punishment or in excess of the level that is reasonable under the circumstances of each situation. All staff must be trained in the use of approved types of force. As the national survey indicates, a high percentage of jails and prisons provide training in the equipment, techniques, and philosophy regarding the use of force. Many agencies complement this knowledge with training in communications and interpersonal skills, which provides an effective array of critical skills related to intervention prior to force. Compared to previous years, today's officer is far better prepared to manage inmate populations safely and effectively.

Types of Force

The following pages are designed to give the reader examples of the types of force typically used in corrections, progressing from the least amount of force to higher forms. Such progression is called the "force continuum," and it is primarily a graphic display of types of force on a sliding scale. There are many different types of continuums in the profession, and this presentation is not provided as necessarily the only version.

In earlier years there was no guidance, equipment, or formal training in using force. The continuum has been the answer to those needs.

However, too often, it has been interpreted to mean that the officer exhausts the lowest level-of-force option, then moves to the next level until it is clearly inadequate, and on up the scale until the level of force properly matches the level of risk and resistance presented by the inmate. Unfortunately, the real world of corrections does not exist that way. Often, the level of risk changes in less than a second, and the appropriateness of force options depends on a number of circumstances. Such direction and specificity may lead to confusion and indecision, which can be unnecessarily dangerous for all involved in high-risk conditions.

Some continuums may be extended to matrixes where force options are on a scale on one side and the level and type of resistance provided by inmates is on the other, resulting in a number of choices within each box. Unfortunately, many officers do not have time to check the matrix under very difficult conditions and must make an immediate and reasonable judgment that could select force anywhere on the scale. The continuum and matrixes are excellent teaching graphics. However, the officer must feel confident to act immediately and know that reasonable, on the spot decisions, will be supported by the department.

Officer Presence

The lowest level of nonphysical force exercised in gaining inmate compliance is the presence of officers among the inmate population. The continuous appearance of properly uniformed, competent staff are always an influence on an inmate's decision to resist direction or act inappropriately. The presence of staff, and their specific numbers, have been the basis of many debates concerning appropriate staffing levels in jails and prisons. In addition to having enough staff to accomplish the concrete work tasks in an area, the need for additional staff presence to provide attention directly to inmate conduct on an ongoing basis is ignored too often. The causes of many correctional disasters have included the absence of officers in inmate work, living, and program areas.

Experience has demonstrated that wherever you leave inmates unsupervised, dangerous contraband makes an appearance. Then, inmates begin to compete for informal leadership, and the area becomes a location for inmates to conduct illegal activities, including assault. The inmate's perception of the officer's authority and power can be enough to change offender behavior.

For example, even under minimum-security conditions where inmate crews work in public areas, staff supervision must be present, professional, and alert at all times for signs that inmate behavior is beginning to deteriorate. Where staff supervision has been inadequate, inmates have assaulted one another, attempted to make contact for drug trafficking, escaped, and otherwise conducted themselves inappropriately in public. Often it is good strategy to provide a strong showing of officer presence, supplemented with video cameras, at the scene where inmates may contemplate aggressive behavior.

Verbal Direction

This next level of nonphysical force is the verbal direction by an officer that requires compliance from an inmate. Many difficult situations may be resolved by good communication skills, problem-solving strategies, verbal direction properly delivered, methods of approaching hostile inmates, de-escalation techniques, and acute sensitivity to early warning signs of problems among inmates.

Much of the success of this method lies in the officer being able to provide communication without further escalating an already tense condition. An example is when two officers observed a classroom of inmates through windows when some of the inmates began to argue very aggressively over an issue in front of the instructor. At first, it was important that the inmates observed the officers through the window. As the intensity of the arguing heightened and the instructor appeared concerned, the officers moved closer to the window. Finally, one of the officers stepped into the classroom and politely asked if everything were okay. Additionally, the officer suggested that if things were getting too hot, the inmates could take a time out and return to their cells for a cooling down period. The suggestions were presented politely as options, not threats. The discussion resulted in an effective de-escalation, and the classroom returned to normal with appreciation from the instructor.

Often an officer can enter a crowd of disruptive inmates and gain control and cooperation with a loud, aggressive tone of voice without offending inmates. On the other hand, a few well-chosen words may diffuse potentially aggressive inmates and may prevent the crowd from forming in the first place. Usually this type of officer is experienced, well respected by the inmates, and he or she does not personalize their communication to any specific person or group.

Empty-Handed Control (Soft/Hard)

This is the first level of physical force available to an officer. There are two kinds of empty-handed control that are designed to overcome resistance. Soft empty-handed control is used for overcoming low levels of resistance. Techniques that fall into this category are pain compliance techniques, joint locks, and leverage locks. Handcuffing without resistance normally is not considered a use of force. When intervening among fighting inmates, often the officer's touch at this level is a signal to inmates to break, and they will submit to open-handed control. Under these conditions, inmates have made their point, had enough, and it is a legitimate behavior in the eyes of everyone to stop fighting and allow themselves to be removed to a more secure area.

Hard empty-handed control is used for overcoming higher levels of resistance including active aggression. Techniques in this category include using neck restraints, cuffing with resistance, and activating pressure points around the head and neck. Usually, neck restraints involving the carotid artery or sleeper holds specifically are prohibited. Under these circumstances, the fighting or the acting out inmate will not lessen the level of aggression and may appear to be escalating. He or she clearly is not willing to submit to control, and may have a weapon. Under these conditions, where lethal force is not justified, correctional officers must be quick to move to hard empty-handed control or intermediate levels of force. Under these conditions, the possibility is extremely high for serious injury to the officer from punches, kicks, or blows from a weapon.

In subduing a fighting or aggressive inmate, it is easy to underestimate strength and emotion where the situation suddenly has escalated beyond immediate capabilities. An example involved two officers who were summoned to a food preparation area in the facility kitchen where two inmates were fighting. As the officers attempted to gain control, they soon realized their efforts were having no effect. At the same time, both inmates grabbed kitchen utensils and seriously wounded one of the two officers with a laceration to the head before control was achieved. The officers underestimated the situation as they entered. They misjudged the intensity of the fight and did not back away when they appeared to be losing ground. They ultimately were successful but not without serious injury. Those judgments are difficult to make.

Intermediate Control Devices (Soft/Hard)

The second level of physical force available to staff members are intermediate control devices. This type of force also has two categories: soft and hard. When the degree of force that can be applied by empty-handed control alone appears to be inadequate and lethal force is not justified, additional physical force through the use of intermediate control devices may be used.

Examples of soft intermediate control devices are Oleoresin Capsicum (OC) handheld aerosols, electronic restraint devices (handheld devices, riot shields, Tasers, and restraint belts), and disabling foam. These sorts of control devices would have been reasonable to use in the kitchen incident described previously.

Hard intermediate devices are impact weapons, such as riot batons, water hoses, hand-thrown grenades, 37 mm gas and projectile launchers, J sticks, expandable batons, or chemical agents such as OC, CS, or CN gas delivered through devices such as the Ispra Projecto Jet or Pepperfogger.

These types of weapons most often are used in an incident such as the following. In the mid-1980s, a new midwestern prison had been open for approximately a year. Yet, management had not fostered staff/inmate dialog, and there was little problem solving. Not surprisingly, inmate discontent erupted into a rebellion during the midday. The cellblocks, administrative area, inmate service area, and workshop areas surrounded a large interior compound. Inmates began gathering in large groups in the compound and refused to go to lockdown. Inmates started breaking windows and destroying equipment in the gymnasium area. Emergency response teams were activated, and the special tactical team was mobilized to come to the facility from locations across the state.

The emergency response teams appeared in the compound with full protective gear and riot batons. The special tactical team provided rooftop lethal support and began to organize a containment area for inmates under restraint. The emergency response team moved across the compound in formation while releasing handheld chemical grenades. The inmates dispersed, submitted to restraint, and were escorted to the containment area. The operation went well in that there were only minor injuries and no lethal force was necessary. Unfortunately, these types of incidents are the worst case scenarios and may not always end without the serious, negative effects on the staff, inmates, and the organization.

All previously discussed types of force are considered nonlethal and must be first considered before lethal force can be used. Nonlethal force should be used to:

1. Stop potentially dangerous and unlawful behavior
2. Protect the staff member or another from injury or death
3. Support the process of implementing lawful orders when the offender offers resistance

As the national survey indicates, most uses of force occur in the housing, recreation, or eating areas. Many of those incidents begin with officers breaking up a fight among inmates. Few correctional officers can forget the experience of entering a dining hall or cellblock where inmates have begun to fight. The noise usually is deafening. Large numbers of inmates have gathered around and are yelling at the fighters and officers. Many of the inmates are encouraging violence towards the officers. At any moment, many decisions must be made. As officer training and instinct begin to guide officers' decisions and actions, some conditions must be determined immediately. Most are covered in procedure and training. The following are some examples:

Are there weapons involved?

Are there back-up officers available?

Is the area being sealed off from the remainder of the facility?

When should staff engage the fighters?

Once the available staff engage the fighters, some further decisions need to be made:

- Should verbal commands fail, is empty-handed restraint appropriate or should intermediate control devices be used?

- Should cuffing restraints be applied in the area for moving the fighters elsewhere, or should they be applied after removing the combatants from the area?

Normally, the best strategy is to remove the fighters from the area with empty-handed restraint and apply cuffing restraints for moving them to isolation areas. It is important to remember that often inmates who at first are passive after separation from the fight later become very aggressive and require further application of empty-handed restraint in order for the officer to continue safely escorting the inmate to an isolation cell.

During the entire time of the incident, staff must assess whether the incident is capable of producing a higher level of resistance. During those times, it is easy to sense the risk to all persons involved. It is also normal to experience fear and be distracted by the surrounding behavior of inmates. Officers must be well prepared to control those emotions and to focus steadily on the most immediate tasks to be performed.

Firearms

This is the highest level of force. Unless a person's life is imminently threatened, it is only to be used after other force alternatives have been considered, or tried, and are found to be ineffective. Firearms may deliver both lethal and nonlethal charges. Nonlethal ammunition is likely to be in the form of gas and smoke delivery rounds, rubberized projectiles, baton, or bird shot rounds. Such ammunition, properly used, lowers the weapon to the hard intermediate level.

Lethal ammunition commonly includes a high-power rifle for both perimeter and sniper weapons. Shotgun lethal ammunition includes rifle slugs and buckshot. Pistols are either revolvers or semi-automatic. Some ammunition is characterized as duty or qualification ammunition. Some jurisdictions use highly sophisticated weapons and munitions such as automatic rifles and explosive devices for specialized tactical purposes.

Lethal force should be used when there are no other alternatives to preventing a loss of life or a serious breach of security, such as escape or dangerous destruction of property, and all other lesser types of force are judged inadequate. Where possible, a warning should be given prior to the use of lethal force. Policy should be specific about warning shots and specifically exclude warning shots in communities. Guidelines should be provided, which clearly indicate areas where warning shots may be fired, such as specific soft dirt locations on perimeters. Lethal force should be used for the following reasons:

1. To prevent escape from a high-security institution

2. To defend oneself or others against an imminent threat of serious bodily injury or imminent danger of death

3. To prevent damage or destruction of property when the loss of the property would directly lead to an escape or attempted escape, grievous bodily harm, or death

Policy specifically should provide limits. Policy should allow firearms to be discharged where the target is clear and not mixed with the position of others in the line of fire.

When considering the circumstances of the fighting incident described previously, it is easy to understand that by the existence of a few additional ingredients, conditions easily could escalate to a higher level of emergency. Should the two fighters represent rival gangs that currently are experiencing disputes, the fighters easily could be joined by other inmates, elevating the incident from a fight to a riot. As the most important strategy is employed, isolation of the area from the remainder of the facility, it is easy to imagine that correctional officers quickly could become hostages.

During these moments, facility staff must be considering higher levels of force and the implementation of the facility's emergency plan, including the deployment of emergency response teams. Strategies then broaden to include issues such as dispersing rioting crowds, continuing the isolation of affected areas, the restraining and confining of rioters, involving of outside agencies, and applying of lethal force where imminent danger exists of death or serious bodily injury. All of these decisions may have to be made in a manner of seconds or minutes under extreme pressure. The circumstances described are not uncommon in the day-to-day conditions in prisons or jails. When considering these conditions, it is easy to comprehend the need for good instincts in correctional officers that are shaped by specialized training and equipment.

Extended Use of Restraints

In the face of extremely threatening or dangerous conduct by inmates, where there exists appropriate policy and practice, it sometimes is reasonable to manage inmates in restraints for prolonged periods of time. Under no circumstances should inmates be subject to extended use of restraint using security-type restraint equipment (handcuffs, belly-chains, leg irons, and so forth). Clinic restraints (canvas, rubber, or leather strapping related to four-point beds and similar devices) only should be used for those purposes. Under no circumstances should inmates be subject to use of restraints as punishment for any reason. Without the proper checks and balances in policy, punishment too often is disguised as the need for control.

The frequency of resorting to this type of force varies depending on the type of the inmate population at each correctional facility. Most commonly it is used to manage self-destructive behavior. Commonly, enraged inmates who are confined to their cells may try anything to be self-destructive, including behavior such as head banging, eye gouging, hanging, or cutting themselves with any object they can find. Makeshift approaches such as taping their hands (they often injure themselves with metallic restraints), or trying to persuade them to wear a protective helmet are seldom successful. Under those circumstances, the use of specially designed restraining equipment is a welcome relief to everyone and major assistance in insuring the safety of the inmate. Since this is a highly aggressive measure to control inmate behavior, it normally is accompanied by strict procedure, very specific documentation, and frequent supervisory reviews at multiple authority levels. Although this procedure usually involves all inmate management staff, depending on the preference of the jurisdiction, the process may be directed by either security personnel or clinical services staff.

Policy covering the prolonged use of restraints must include the type of restraint to be used. Soft restraints in the form of plastic or leather must be the choice where more long-term, aggressive behavior is anticipated. The restraints can be attached to a bed specially designed for that purpose or the inmate can be left in a cell where the restraints are not attached to a stationary fixture.

All the specifics with respect to prolonged periods of placing inmates in restraint must be expressed in policy. The following are some important elements recommended for inclusion. The condition of the inmate in restraint must be such that critical functions such as breathing, blood circulation, and any other medical concerns related to each inmate under restraint are fully addressed. Both medical and security staff must provide and document frequent reviews and evaluations of the inmate's condition. Mental health personnel should provide direction or consulting advice on the decision to restrain, provide status evaluations, and be consulted on the decision to remove restraints. The initial decision to restrain, and subsequent decisions to restrain for prolonged periods of time, must be authorized by the shift commander or higher. Extended periods of restraint (four to eight hours) must be approved by departmental executive staff. As with all applications of all authorized force, correctional staff involved in the use of restraints for a prolonged period of time must be fully trained in the procedure.

Specialized Teams

Correctional staff must be prepared to use levels of force appropriate for the type and extent of inmate resistance presented by each situation. Some duty posts are assigned a weapon as in control rooms, towers, and transportation vehicles. Under other conditions, staff must be prepared to use lesser levels of force at any time during the operation of a correctional facility. Many jurisdictions have specialized teams of staff who exercise the use of force under specific, nonroutine conditions. As with force continuums, there are a variety of configurations throughout the profession. The following three sections describe examples of those organizations.

Forced Cell Entry Teams

The use of forced cell entry teams has not always been a common practice in corrections. Years ago, staff were not trained. There was little or no protective equipment, including intermediate control devices. Staff improvised cell entries, with the resulting high incidence of staff and inmate injury. Current practice is much more effective, and safer for everyone involved. Forced cell entries are typically more common in facilities that manage high risk, aggressive offenders or in those facilities that are not being effective in using other, nonphysical means for solving problems with offenders.

More recently, agencies have resorted to using OC (Oleo Capsicum Resin), after all verbal attempts to resolve problems have failed, prior to the order for the forced cell entry team to enter the cell. Sometimes the team is held in reserve, out of sight of the inmate, while the OC is being administered. For the inmates, the drama of forced cell entry is lost with the use OC. It is no longer seen as an activity for the disruptive inmate's amusement. For those reasons, the use of OCs can reduce the frequency of forced cell entries by as much as 50 percent. Particularly with the advent of transmittal of disease through body fluids, it is important as a policy matter to reduce the chances of violent staff/inmate contact, where possible.

A forced cell entry team is a group (four to six officers) who have been specially trained in providing a preplanned, organized process for gaining cell entry for retrieving a disruptive or noncompliant inmate or to move an inmate through the use of force. The team should be equipped with protective equipment for all members. The team should be qualified and prepared to use the level of nonlethal force that is reasonable to gain compliance from the inmate. Once the team is presented to the inmate, the inmate may become cooperative in response to the presence of the team. Otherwise, the inmate normally is restrained through empty-handed control as the team enters the cell. Most teams will use a reverse curve, Plexiglas shield, or stun shield held by the point person as the team enters the cell. The strategy is to pin the inmate against the cell wall as the remaining team members gain control of the inmate's arms and legs, with each team member responsible for a specific limb.

Typically, forced cell entry is used to prevent an inmate from being self-destructive, to prevent the destruction of property, to move inmates according to administrative or court order, to vacate a cell for operational purposes (sanitation, searches, emergency evacuation, and so forth), and to attend to an ill or unresponsive high-risk inmate. Normally, most forced cell entry experiences occur in high-security environments that contain the most disruptive, high-risk offenders.

Except in emergencies, this process should not take place without the following: extensive efforts to persuade the inmate to comply, videotaping for the record, and permission from a higher authority to proceed. The training for team members should include specific roles of each team member, certified force skills for all devices used, a policy on force, and forced cell entry protocol. Each forced cell entry should be documented in detail and accompanied by the shift commander and medical supervision throughout the event.

Forced cell entry strategy may be complicated. There should be specific plans for overcoming wet or soapy floors, inmate attempts at jamming doors, various kinds of barricades, possible weapons held by the inmate, and methods of insuring insertion of OC into the cell.

Emergency Response Teams

An Emergency Response Team is a designated, specially selected and trained team at each correctional facility or complex that is used to contain and control an emergency (riot, fire, natural disaster, and so forth). Normally, participants are volunteers and are not provided additional compensation for their efforts and commitment. Each team is prepared to use the force that is reasonable in each individual situation. Teams typically are organized according to the level of force they are trained to use. Emergency response teams often are designated as lethal force/weapons teams, riot teams, and cuffing/retention teams. Other specialized teams such as fugitive search, hostage negotiation, and post-trauma treatment may exist in some systems.

Typically, emergency response team requirements under emergency conditions are to do things such as:

1. Disperse groups of rioting inmates

2. Apply all levels of force

3. Conduct searches

4. Provide escorts for staff, inmates, and mutual aid agencies

5. Administer first aid or CPR

---

6. Perform staff welfare checks

7. Supervise inmate holding and triage areas

8. Establish/supervise perimeters

Many emergency response teams have an organizational structure, a role in the departmental emergency plan, membership qualifications, physical fitness requirements, and annual training plans or requirements. The training requirements should include certification in all areas of force and emergency medical services that may be used by the team.

Specialized Tactical Teams

A specialized tactical team is a designated, specially selected and trained team (such as a SORT or SWAT team), which usually services an entire system to contain and control special types of emergencies. Normally, participants are volunteers from facilities across the jurisdiction. The team is highly trained in specialized applications of force. Some systems organize teams by regions or each team has a single capability. Examples of performance requirements under actual emergency conditions are armed building clearing, sniper operations, armed transport for high-risk operations, hostage retrieval, and special security operations.

Like emergency response team organizations, special tactical teams have an organizational structure, a role in the departmental emergency plan, membership qualifications, physical fitness requirements, and annual training plans or requirements. The training requirements normally include certification in all areas of force and emergency medical services, including specialized weaponry and tactics such as automatic firearms, explosives, sniper operations, and hostage extractions. It is generally accepted that special tactical team operations employ higher performance and qualification requirements than any other use-of-force team.

Fugitive Search Teams

Many agencies pursue inmates who escape from their custody. The decision to pursue depends on policy and related conditions of local jurisdictions. In many cases, under the fleeing felon rule, correctional staff are permitted to use lethal force in the apprehension of inmate fugitives. The mission and responsibility of the correctional officers in terms of use of force in pursuit of fugitives becomes much the same as for law enforcement personnel.

The possibility of the need to use force exists under a variety of conditions. Fugitive pursuit is most often a highly dramatic experience that can last from a few minutes to many days. It can lead teams through rough terrain, through communities, and requires extensive searches of buildings and homes and contact with the general public. Operations properly assume that a fugitive must be presumed dangerous, providing the possibility that force may have to be used in defense or to assure capture.

Laws and policy usually require that all other reasonable attempts to apprehend have been made, and that a warning be given prior to the use of lethal force. These requirements often leave correctional staff with the impression that much is left to interpretation in after-action reviews of uses of lethal force. However, case law tends to be supportive of correctional officers whose conduct falls within the "reasonable person" framework. Fortunately, most fugitives will submit to custody upon hearing a warning in the form of a shout or the discharge of a weapon.

Some of the major challenges in operating fugitive search teams are as follows: the training requirements needed for team members include specialty skills not normally taught by correctional agencies (inmate tracking, dog handling, building searches, advanced weapons training, roadblock operations, and so forth). Oftentimes, agencies experience difficulty in achieving the resources to provide this type of training to all search team members.

When correctional officers are in pursuit of fugitives beyond the boundaries of prison property, it is absolutely essential to operate within the parameters of agreements with affected governing agencies. Jurisdictions vary with respect to correctional agencies being empowered to pursue. Dictated by statute or constitution, county emergencies often are conducted under the authority of the sheriff. Therefore, fugitive pursuit must be conducted through an understanding with the sheriff as the commander of the operation. Typically, rural sheriffs welcome the willingness of the correctional agency to pursue their fugitive inmates, and the discharge of a weapon does not raise as much of a concern as would occur in an urban setting. The sheriff should have a detailed agreement with the correctional agency concerning the search in regards to road-blocks, road/highway patrolling, notifications, communications, private property, building searches, and use of lethal force. Urban settings are much more complicated, and urban municipalities are more likely to manage apprehension of fugitives without the assistance of correctional staff.

Planned Use of Force

Staff must be expected to apply force immediately at any time during the course of performing their work. There are times that they must react suddenly. Some examples are breaking up fights, encountering an inmate who becomes angry, aggressive, and unwilling to comply with direction, or moving or transporting inmates under restraint. Other times, the inmate is isolated and the immediate area is secure, allowing the passage of time to support further attempts at resolution or to allow valuable time to plan and coordinate the use of force.

Planned uses of force helps insure a greater degree of success and safety at the conclusion of the incident. All planned uses of force should be coordinated with a higher authority, be videotaped for the clearest possible record of the event, accompanied by extensive nonphysical efforts to resolve the issue, and there should be medical staff in attendance throughout the process.

Force Deployment

Generally, force deployment should be a practiced system that each agency operates based on a balance between the perception of risk presented by inmates and the need to secure force-related equipment properly. The majority of agencies keep storage of weapons, munitions, and emergency response team equipment in a secure space outside the facility perimeters. Storage spaces and systems should be arranged to achieve maximum efficiency in quickly deploying equipment to authorized staff.

There are a variety of approaches among agencies. Many facilities operate satellite storage spaces within the facility for faster deployment of equipment. Some operate posts with lethal weapons capability on perimeters, in interior yard spaces, and even in housing unit control rooms. Some agencies allow officers to carry intermediate control devices

(J-sticks, OC canisters, electronic control devices, and so forth) inside the facility on a routine basis. Others require that the equipment be drawn from a protected storage space when needed. For example, in one major urban jail system, emergency response team equipment is stored on a cart that is kept in a secure location. Under emergency conditions, it is wheeled to the general area before staff draw their equipment and begin to address the emergency.

All systems should include steps for checking out and returning weapons to storage spaces. In high-risk areas, it is important to remember that an inmate can inflict mortal wounds with a homemade knife or a blunt object in a matter of seconds. Those sorts of assaults are not uncommon, and lives can be saved by quick, professional deployment of force. On the other hand, others may argue that too much dependence on use of force causes the focus to shift away from critical inmate management activities, such as communication, dialog, or face-to-face problem solving. Each side of the discussion should realize that both approaches are compatible and may coexist as an effective approach to managing inmate populations.

Philosophy on Use of Force

Being effective in terms of detecting and solving problems prior to the need for force is the duty and responsibility of all correctional professionals. When those efforts fail, use of force is a very important short-term fix, but it must never be relied on as a long-term solution to challenges in managing inmates.

The correctional officer must not allow a competition of egos to interfere with effectively dealing with disruptive inmates. Backing down, de-escalating the situation, reducing the possibility for conflict is the goal of the officer and must not be regarded as "losing face." It should be understood that doing so is not a loss to the officer, but a compliment in having constructively restored control and safety to the facility. Effective regulation of use of force is difficult, if not impossible, without substantial support and modeling of the appropriate philosophy by staff in leadership positions.

All uses of force must be performed professionally, using only the amount and type of force that is reasonable under the circumstances to insure safety and control throughout each facility or detention center. Force must never be used as retribution. Due to the high stress conditions found in corrections on a day-to-day basis, it often is tempting for correctional officers to personalize insults and failures in managing difficult inmates. It is critical that those impressions not affect the officer's demeanor in engaging with the inmate. Personal reprisal must never be used against inmates, nor allowed to affect the decision to apply and use force. Staff always must have confidence that they are in control and they will win all inmate conflicts involving force with highly trained, objective performance. Where possible, staff who appear personally affected by an inmate's conduct that may lead to a use of force should be removed or replaced for that specific incident.

Inmate populations devote time and energy in determining weaknesses in the staff's ability to maintain control and order in managing the prison environment. The use-of-force program must portray competent, well-equipped, well-trained, confident staff prepared to apply force when the situation requires. It is an important message. Such a condition of readiness is entirely compatible with officers' attempts at solving problems through the use of interpersonal skills. It is a welcome condition for inmates who wish to be assured of their safety. It is a message that further supports the wisdom of peaceful alternatives rather than violent or aggressive means to solve problems.

Implications of the Excessive Use of Force

The courts have assumed that due to the nature of the correctional environment, unregulated, unsupervised uses of force by staff ultimately will become abusive. Staff must be aware of the implications of excessive use of force. Some of the implications of excessive force consistently used in a facility are the following:

1. Staff involved in an excessive use of force may be required to respond to criminal and civil proceedings and are likely to be subject to severe disciplinary action by their agency.

2. Excessive use of force models behavior to other staff, which means that violations of, and inconsistencies in application of laws and rules may be viewed as acceptable within the

organization. Such a condition promotes an unsafe and unpredictable atmosphere for everyone.

3. Excessive use of force models behavior to inmates that communicates a message of acceptance of force as a primary method of solving problems among humans. This message is directly contrary to the mission expressed by most correctional jurisdictions.

4. Excessive use of force may be viewed by staff as an acceptable substitute for the array of interpersonal skills that are critical to effective inmate management.

5. If excessive use of force is used to manage inmate behavior, it is likely to affect staff/inmate dialog in an extremely negative fashion. This condition can distort communication and raise fears and feelings of unpredictability among inmates.

6. Excessive use of force may informally place a perception of power in the hands of participating staff. That power is likely to be inconsistent with the intentions of the formal organization. This condition can create divisive and unhealthy relationships among staff in the form of staff taking sides in terms of those who participate and those who do not. Staff who choose not to participate may appear withdrawn and uncommunicative and may apply for transfer or resign.

7. Excessive use of force easily can combine with other facility problems (ineffective communication, insufficient programs, poor staff morale, and so forth) to ignite an inmate disturbance.

8. When inmates view staff using excessive force, or corporal punishment, they may view their environment as no longer safe to the extent they may be encouraged to take measures to protect themselves.

9. Public knowledge of excessive force incidents is extremely damaging to the image of corrections professionals, to the careers of those involved, and can create long-term regulatory entanglements through courts of law and by human interest groups.

Key Indicators of Excessive Use of Force

The national survey indicates that in all the uses of force reported, there were very few reports of instances when the force used was excessive, and very few disciplinary actions were taken against correctional officers for excessive use of force. It is clear that correctional staff overall are doing an excellent job. However, it does not mean the excessive force and corporal punishment is not occurring. It is critical that correctional leaders remain diligent and proactive in their sensitivity to each use of force within their organization. Part of that process must involve being aware of some of the early warning signs that excessive use of force may be happening in their organization.

Nowhere in corrections does the saying, "where there is smoke, there is fire" apply more than in the review of information on use of force. The following are some indicators that excessive use of force may be occurring. Should any number of these indicators exist, leaders should expend greater effort to examine related incidents at their facility. They are as follows:

1. Staff and/or inmate rumors, incident reports, and inmate grievances may be important indicators. This does not suggest that leadership should react to every individual piece of information. However, when patterns evolve from numerous sources, it is time to take a more serious look.

2. When unexplained injuries occur, they merit careful attention. These injuries must be found to not fit the circumstances. As an example, a forced cell entry is conducted, and it goes well with only moderate resistance on the part of the inmate. However, serious injuries occur that seem excessive under the circumstances. As a result, further examination may be needed. Some examples of those kinds of injuries are deep and extensive lacerations, breaks in large bones (such as the leg or arm), or bruising from hard intermediate weapons, which appear to be excessive for the circumstances or in locations which suggest that the inmate may have been fully restrained at the time the blows were delivered. Where these instances occur in a pattern, serious and immediate examination of the events would be

important. A pattern could be more than two consecutive events in a relatively short period of time.

3. Where there is a an increase in the frequency in the overall uses of force without a reasonable explanation, management should remain concerned until an explanation is achieved. The increase could be overall, or more focused on one shift rather than others.

4. Management should be aware of the idea that where there is a history of burnout and no rotation of staff in facilities that contain high-risk, disruptive inmates, a higher potential exists for excessive use of force.

5. Management should be sensitive to the idea that where staff fail to provide sufficient information, are clearly mimicking one another on incident reports, or are reluctant to discuss conditions surrounding a use of force, a possibility exists that excessive force is being used.

6. Likewise, staff should be sensitive to significant and extreme changes in inmate behavior. Some examples include times when inmate behavior is uncharacteristic, such as when inmates no longer participate in normal communication, larger numbers of inmates are showing up for sick call, there are groupings by race or gang affiliation, and inmates show a significant increase in requests for transfer in jobs or to other facilities. Uncharacteristic behavior also may include normally calm, relaxed inmates become very verbal and aggressive, or those who are normally communicative suddenly withdraw. Under these circumstances, it is important for staff to trust their hunches and make a special effort to communicate with inmates and other staff.

The negative effects on individuals and organizations of a pattern of use of force as corporal punishment can be very difficult to undo. At times, the challenge can assume the dimensions of an attitude change throughout the entire organization. In the most extreme cases, the challenge can be attempting to change a culture of terror in which genuine concern over the welfare of inmates has been replaced by hatred, contempt, and indifference to that of acceptance of a new way of doing business.

Elements of A Successful Use of Force Program

There are several key components of a successful use of force program for correctional institutions and departments. These include, at a minimum, the following which are discussed in turn: administrative oversight, training, policy, and documentation.

Administrative Oversight

All security, emergency, and staff performance systems in corrections must be monitored and supervised continually. Uses of force may be reduced significantly by staff who invest time and energy into analyzing inmate populations with the idea of predicting where problems may occur. Without constant attention, these systems can deteriorate and produce major problems within days or weeks of a change in focus.

Administrative oversight of the use-of-force process must achieve a very clear understanding among staff that the leadership of the organization is supportive and confident in the staff's use of force as a part of their job performance. Staff must know that reasonable use of force is their duty and the right thing to do. Additionally, administrators should encourage staff to be accountable for job performance. This accountability needs to include both tangible support for excellent work, constructive criticism toward improving future performance, and confidence that they will be treated fairly.

The advantages of an effective administrative oversight system are as follows:

- It delivers a critical message to the entire facility or department and the public, indicating that each use-of-force incident is an extremely important event that it takes seriously, and the related oversight is an expression of that importance.

- It provides a written history of force incidents, which serves as educational information, a security performance measurement or indicator, and protection from legal and administrative actions.

- It provides an opportunity for management to express support and confidence in staff performance when they use force.

82

The essential elements of administrative oversight include the following seven items:

1. The administrative review is both openly complimentary towards excellent staff performance in the use of force and provides constructive direction for improvement, where appropriate.

2. All staff and witnesses to uses of force produce a written statement, and the staff involved are interviewed as part of the administrative review. An additional, standardized use-of-force report should be completed to accompany the staff statements. The ACA national survey indicates that only 59 percent of the state corrections departments require a formal, written statement, and only 53 percent require an interview with the officer(s) involved. Without full participation of officers in the use-of-force review, the importance of the process is seriously diminished.

3. It involves a review at multiple points within the agency. At a minimum, it should include the shift commander, an administrative officer, the administrative head of the facility (such as a warden or superintendent), and at least one executive level person from the central agency administration (for example, an inspector general, a deputy director of institutions, or a chief of security operations). One level should include a formal review with formal, taped interviews with involved staff, examinations of all documents, videotapes, and related information. This review should conclude with a formal report and findings to the administrative head of the facility. All information should be shared and discussed with the staff involved in the interest of improvement and professional development. The administrative head of the facility should review the information and formally declare in writing that the amount and type of force used was appropriate for the circumstances. If it was not appropriate, then the appropriate follow-up corrective actions should be a part of the documentation. The remainder of the reviews should be informal with questions and requests for clarification addressed to the administrative head of the facility.

4. The information reported on the use-of-force information report should be standardized and support a larger system of data gathering. Some types of information might be frequency of force incidents by facility, department, shift, and so forth. That information must be used by correctional management to track critical trends or characteristics on force. The results should guide the design of future training, application of resources, and strategic plans.

5. Administrative review should provide aggressive outcome for excessive uses of force in terms of disciplinary and corrective actions. These should be implemented when staff clearly use force in a malicious manner, solely designed to bring harm to the inmate. Accountability includes clear, predictable consequences for wrongful actions. These kinds of decisions are always difficult and must be made in light of all the circumstances. However, the outcome must provide a clear message to all that such acts will not be tolerated under any circumstances.

6. The administrative oversight must have integrity in that each incident is viewed with the same level of seriousness and attention to detail. The process must never be viewed as a rubber-stamp exercise.

7. The administrative oversight process must be clearly expressed in policy.

Training

Force cannot be used successfully without extensive staff training. A few years ago in a midwestern state, inmates in a close-custody portion of a prison created a disturbance. During the process of bringing the incident under control, several staff were injured. Afterwards, one of the uninjured staff was being interviewed by the media. Someone asked what contributed most to remaining injury free. He immediately responded by saying his safety was a result of instinct shaped by training that guided his actions during the disturbance. It seemed to him as though his actions were automatic.

As the survey indicates, most agencies train staff in use-of-force philosophy, equipment, and techniques. There are several outcomes that use-of-force training must achieve. First, and most importantly, training must cause staff performance, in terms of the use of force and related decision making, to be consistent with policy and procedure. This must be done to the extent that appropriate staff performance is second nature and that staff feel a high level of confidence in their ability to perform under a variety of circumstances.

Second, use-of-force training must educate so that, in addition to competency with equipment and techniques, staff must become knowledgeable in use-of-force policy and, as described in the survey, it shapes staff thinking. It is sometimes said that attitude is everything and there is no place where that idea is more important than in use of force in corrections. The training forum is the most effective tool for setting the tone for the professional use of force. That tone setting must address the "code of silence" in terms of outlining the legal liability of staff for not reporting acts of excessive use of force. Additionally, the negative effects on the organization discussed earlier should be reviewed.

Third, the training experience must provide staff with confidence that they have the full support and encouragement of the agency when they use force as part of their job performance. At the same time, they must accept being accountable for any acts of wanton, malicious behavior as a part of a use-of-force incident. Clear teaching and presentation must invite the officer to be comfortable with the concept that reasonable conduct in the use of force is achievable in every situation, is the right thing to do, and will be supported by the agency and the legal system.

In addition to the survey results on training as it relates to the implementation of force policy, the following are important points:

1. Training in use of force needs to provide explanations of important definitions such as physical force, control, resistance, and corporal punishment. Departments should include their definitions of these terms in their use-of-force policies. Correctional officers need to have the same understandings and use the same terminology when referring to force issues.

2. The training needs to include various methods of relating the levels and types of force to the levels and degree of risk and resistance presented by the inmate. The force continuum is a graphics tool to demonstrate how force options change with the rising or lowering of risk and resistance presented by the inmate. The misconception created by this device is, since the continuum is presented as a sliding scale, that corrections staff are obligated to attempt to perform or extensively consider all lower levels of force options prior to the application of the appropriate level of force. This point of view, compounded by vivid emphasis on legal liability, may cause officers to be more hesitant rather than decisive in proceeding to the correct force option. Training must help staff achieve confidence, and feel comfortable going directly to the best force option for the circumstances.

Train like u Fight

The more u sweat in peace the less u bleed during a war

3. The more closely training imitates the actual job environment, and is participatory in style, the more effective it will be. Live scenarios can be described and assessed among the student group. That process could be enhanced by using video presentations of live or staged events with subsequent discussion and evaluations. Lethal force teams can be trained with "shoot, do not shoot" videos, or with building clearing or hostage extractions staged in actual buildings. Empty-handed restraint is best trained with live demonstrations using protective suits. There are many ways to bring reality to the classroom.

4. Force training should complemented by teaching the interpersonal skills that are important in de-escalating an angry, volatile situation with inmates before use of force is deemed necessary.

5. Force training should provide some direction and coaching for those who have not experienced approaching tense situations where force may be required. Some coaching related to the importance of overcoming normal fears and adrenaline flows to remain focused is important for all staff.

6. It is important not to forget the importance of informal training through supervisory and peer group mentoring, including the

educational value of after-action analysis of actual incidents. Very often, effective strategies vary depending on the local facility architecture and inmate population dynamics.

7. A minimum level of use-of-force skills must be assured for each student who completes training. This should be expressed in terms of proficiency in the use of equipment in live testing scenarios and comprehension displayed in written and oral testing.

8. Staff must be trained to understand that the code of silence is prohibited by policy, and the law requires that all involved in and witnesses to uses of force provide a detailed, written report before leaving duty. Administrators must stress that failure to report will be treated as a possible criminal offense and will be regarded as willful, unprofessional conduct worthy of severe discipline or dismissal.

Policy

With the tremendous growth and expansion in corrections in the last two decades, correctional agencies, for the most part, have become large organizations that cannot afford to operate a collection of facilities as though each were an independent element with freedom of decision making on all issues. Nowhere is that condition more compelling than on the issues related to the use of force. The most critical tool in a standardized approach is policy. Policy is the cornerstone of all use-of-force programs. Policy should shape attitude, drive training curricula, describe processes, outline duties, and describe reporting obligations and procedures. Policy should require that each use-of-force incident be debriefed, and that the conclusions of administrative reviews be shared with staff. Chapter 6, "Developing and Implementing a Use-of-force Policy," details the essential elements of a use-of-force policy.

Documentation

All uses of force should be documented thoroughly by all involved participants or witnesses, whether as a participant or witness. The information provided then comprises the complete historical record of each use-of-force event. All officers should be required to complete an incident report covering the basics of who, what, where, and when before they leave at the end of their shift. That information, along with a medical examination report, photographs, and videotapes, should be attached to a standardized, consolidated report form that is copied up through the chain of command.

That form should include critical information such as the identity of the inmate, reason for the use of force, whether a medical examination has been completed, a description of the inmates' actions, level of force used, and names of staff and inmate witnesses. Related to the administrative oversight process mentioned earlier, it is essential that the administrative head of the facility declare in writing whether the type and amount of force used was appropriate under the circumstances.

Force Technology

The array of choices related to correctional use-of-force equipment has broadened significantly in the past years. Recent trends are mostly in the direction of weapons, which limit physical contact, are low impact, and in most cases, are less than lethal in effect. Improvements in force technology, along with serious efforts at evaluation and selection of equipment, have provided staff with the tools they need to get the job done while minimizing injury and preserving a high degree of safety for everyone.

Because correctional agencies have experienced tremendous periods of growth in the recent past, it has become necessary to standardize force options and related technologies for the sake of efficiency in terms of costs, effectiveness, staff training needs, and operations simplicity. All equipment selected for use should be officially approved by the department executive staff. Choices should be a part of thoughtful, long-term planning that considers such factors as reliability, proven performance, and legal history. The selection process should include the participation of correctional staff who are experienced in the use of force.

Some examples of use-of-force technology that are currently available include the following:

1. Electrified perimeter barriers

2. Radio communication systems for tactical convenience

3. Improved gas masks and riot helmets

4. Improved chemical weapons and delivery systems

5. Specialized ordnance such as flashbang, stingball rounds, and ricochet-proof ammunition

6. Handheld and specialized electronic control devices

7. New and better types of body armor

8. Disabling foams

9. New and better types of restraint devices

10. Infrared vision for towers and perimeter vehicles

11. Delivery of control chemicals by high-intensity water stream both into prison cells and over long distances

Choices of equipment are driven by staff preference, budget, and legal issues. Making such choices are not easy decisions in the face of the multitude of vendors and alternatives offered today.

Conclusion

In this chapter, we have discussed both the types of force and use-of-force techniques commonly applied in today's prisons and the philosophy underlying the use of force in corrections. It is important to remember that competent use of force involves not just knowing how to use the various use-of-force techniques, but also knowing how not to use more force than is required to regain control of a situation.

Professional correctional officers must be skilled communicators and problem solvers. Working with inmates requires the ability to control and diffuse tense situations and avoid unnecessary escalation of conflict. The use of force is, as we stated earlier, situational. This means correctional officers must know how to use the least amount of force appropriate in a given situation. This requires the ability to assess a situation quickly and accurately, as well as training in conflict management.

The best way to ensure correctional officers use only the appropriate amount of force is to provide them with training in both: (1) use-of-force techniques and equipment, and (2) use-of-force philosophy. Training in use-of-force techniques and equipment is fairly straightforward and involves familiarizing correctional personnel with the methods of applying force and the technology used in various situations. Training in use-of-force philosophy is a little more complicated and involves exposing correctional personnel to the legal and ethical requirements imposed on them.

The reality is that it is far easier to teach staff how to use a restraint technique or a weapon than it is to teach them how to gain control of a confrontational situation using the least amount of force necessary without endangering themselves or others. This involves training on the use-of-force continuum, as well as training in communication and problem-solving techniques.

The use of force is an unavoidable part of the corrections profession. While it cannot be avoided, proper training in the techniques of conflict resolution and the appropriate degree of force can ensure that only as much force as is absolutely necessary to maintain control is used. This is the goal of the professional correctional officer.

Developing and Implementing a Use-of-force Policy

Darrell L. Ross, Ph.D.

Introduction

Working in a contemporary correctional facility requires much of today's correctional officer. The officer is on the front line enforcing laws and departmental policy in an environment that is frequently hostile and violent. Daily, the officer makes split-second decisions that affect inmates' lives and their own welfare. Correctional officers regularly are required to make decisions regarding the use of force. Whether it involves breaking up a fight between prisoners, using force in self-defense, or deciding to use some type of force equipment, officers must exercise judgment and discretion in their decision to use force, recognizing there is a privilege given to use reasonable force to accomplish a lawful objective.

Officers must bear in mind the use of force beyond what is reasonably required in a particular situation may render the officer liable for damages in a civil lawsuit or, more likely, violate agency policy and expose the officer to discipline and possibly termination of employment.

Correctional administrators also may face liability. Administrators may be held liable for failing to develop and implement use-of-force policies, and for failing to train officers in the proper limits of using force, if it can be demonstrated that this failure constitutes "deliberate indifference."

A great deal of civil litigation involving correctional officers and supervisors has emerged from the use of force since the erosion of the "hands-off doctrine" in the late 1960s. Ross (1997) conducted a content analysis of 3,200 published Title 42 U.S.C. Section 1983 prisoner lawsuits filed between 1970 and 1994. Correctional officials prevailed in 51 percent of prisoner claims of excessive force (215 cases) and lost 59 percent of the litigation involving administrative liability (241 cases).

Common issues on which correctional officials have lost include deficient policy, lack of policies and procedures, failure to train, failure to direct, or failure to supervise employees. Moreover, correctional officers were named as defendants in approximately 33 percent of the total claims, while administrators were named in 20 percent of the cases. Both administrators and officers were named in 39 percent of the litigation.

Hanson and Daley (1995) reviewed 2,700 Section 1983 cases filed by inmate plaintiffs in 9 states in 1992. They found 21 percent of the prisoners' litigation were issues of physical security, which included claims of excessive force. Their study also revealed that correctional officers were named as defendants in 26 percent of the cases, while 22 percent of the litigation named an administrator as a defendant. They also found that while correctional officers and administrators were frequently named as defendants, in 94 percent of the cases, the defendant officers and administrators were found not liable.

In 1992, the U.S. Supreme Court issued an important decision in a use-of-force case. In *Hudson v. McMillian* (1992) two correctional officers beat a restrained prisoner with a supervisor present. A lower court found the officers used excessive force. The Supreme Court agreed with the lower court and established the standard by which to determine liability: "whether the force was applied in a good faith effort to maintain or restore discipline, or maliciously and sadistically to cause harm." The ruling created a ripple effect for correctional administrators with regard to reevaluating or revising their use of force policies, policy implementation, training in force policy, and acceptable force control measures. Moreover, this case demonstrates the necessity of supervisory accountability in controlling and directing subordinates in this high liability topic.

The purpose of this chapter is to describe a systematic strategy for developing and implementing a solid and legally defensible use-of-force policy in correctional agencies. The discussion addresses legal implications of policy development, the role of agency policy, and provides recommendations for structuring and implementing a use-of-force policy. Managing the use of force by correctional officers and administrators is one of the most important challenges facing correctional departments today. The way in which officers enforce facility regulations to protect themselves and prisoners can be problematic. Hence, policy and guidelines must be developed to assist officers in making justifiable decisions for using force and to help reduce the department's risk of litigation.

A policy in and of itself cannot prevent an inmate's lawsuit. What is needed, however, is a current policy which directs officers' judgment and use-of-force decision making, which justifies a course of action, and which provides a legal framework in which officers perform their duties. This provides a basis for officer/department defense in a lawsuit and provides a mechanism for force analysis in the context of the force confrontation. Administrators should adopt a proactive position both in developing and maintaining a use-of-force policy. Failure to implement a comprehensive force policy in clear and unequivocal terms could be construed as ignoring administrative responsibilities and being deliberately indifferent to the constitutional rights of prisoners.

Legal Necessity of Policy

The management issues concerning how correctional officers confront potentially dangerous situations, in terms of clear policy, control measures, and training can be problematic. The decision to use force in varying situations is a crucial one, especially in an environment that takes advantage of those who either under react or overreact. Accordingly, it is paramount that correctional officers act within legal guidelines, ethics, good judgment, and accepted practices and are prepared adequately to act wisely whenever using force in the course of their duties. The development and implementation of workable and professionally correct policies and procedures are necessary for the efficient and effective operation of any correctional organization.

While governmental agencies may not be sued directly under Section 1983, suits may be brought against agency chief administrators in their official capacity. Generally, in an action filed in accordance with Section 1983 against a correctional entity, the plaintiff will make the following allegations (del Carmen, 1991):

- That there is or was a policy promulgated by the agency policymaker

- That the policy caused the injury to the plaintiff

- That the injury constituted a violation of the plaintiff's constitutional rights

Governmental liability ensues when the inmate's constitutional rights are violated stemming from "official policy." Official policy normally means an adopted and promulgated statement by the agency's head who has the authority to develop policy. Included in this are activities so common and well settled as to constitute a custom that fairly represents agency policy. Not every administrator is categorized as an official policy maker, although a warden and sheriff usually are. This would be determined by state or local law. Although unwritten, a custom may constitute policy, and again this would be a matter to be proven in court.

Several court decisions provide examples of the court's legal interpretation of policy pertaining to excessive force. In the Eleventh Circuit Court of Appeals decision of *Vineyard v. County of Murray*, Georgia (990 F.2d 1207, 1993), the court entered a judgment against deputies and a sheriff for beating an arrestee. The appellate court found evidence, which supported a finding that the officer's deliberate indifference to the detainee's right to be free from excessive force was the key element in the violation of the detainee's constitutional right. The court concluded that the policies of the agency were deficient in directing officers in reporting the use of force.

Policy implications were cited in *Giroux v. Sherman* (807 F. Supp. 1182, E.D. PA. 1992) when the court found eight correctional officers were liable for excessive force when they beat a prisoner on four separate occasions. The court found that the actions of the officers were wanton and without provocation, and implied that training in the use-of-force policy was deficient.

In *Coleman v. Wilson*, (912 F.Supp. 1282, E.D. Cal. 1995), the district court found the use of Tasers against inmates with serious mental disorders caused substantial harm to the inmates. Evidence supported the finding that the policy of handling mentally impaired prisoners was defective and training of officers was inadequate. The three-hour training course for new officers and the in-service course were found to be insufficient to prevent some officers from using punitive measures to control prisoners.

This brief discussion of liability regarding policy illustrates how the agency may be liable if prisoners allege their constitutional rights were violated due to officers failing to act in accordance with policy, or where policy was the moving force. The question which must be answered relative to allegations of policy deficiencies in excessive force claims is, "Was the injury caused by official policy?" If the court agrees, then agency liability will be imposed. The administrative implications become important as agency heads must keep their policies current with the changing law, train officers to them, and insure supervisors enforce the proper implementation of policies.

The Role of Departmental Policy

The term "policy" has been used in a variety of ways and definitions of what constitutes a policy are numerous. Eulau and Prewitt (1973) define policy as a standing decision characterized by behavioral consistency and repetitiveness on part of both those who make it and those who abide by it. In this manner, policy is observed as the end result of the decision-making process, and certain responsibilities exist for those who develop policy and those who carry it out. Certo (1985) defines policy as a standing plan that furnishes broad, general guidelines for channeling management thinking toward taking action consistent with reaching organizational objectives. In this case, policy is related to the achievement of organizational mission and goals. Archambeault and Archambeault

(1982) broadly define policy as any statement or set of statements that are written, expressed verbally, or presumed operative that outline the goals, objectives, purpose, scope, principles of organization and operational values, beliefs, and ideology, and that justify the continued existence of that organization.

Houston (1995) defines policy as general philosophical principles that guide development of strategies and programs on behalf of the agency. He further states that a "good" policy is one that accomplishes one or several of the following:

1. It attempts to correct a past error in policy, which is referred to as fine tuning.

2. It attempts to prevent future errors in policy by articulating the policy formulator's thinking and attempts to channel future thinking on a subject.

3. It clarifies numerous and different goals, separates competing goals, and/or brings to light previously unidentified goals.

4. It enables the organization to accomplish its stated goals.

The role of policy in a correctional agency indicates to the public where an agency stands on major issues while concomitantly providing the agency with a set of standards for which it can be held accountable (Gamire, 1985). Policy is a means by which organizations guide the actions and decisions of employees. Policies establish priorities, define ethical behavior, set standards for personnel evaluation and promotion, outline and define job tasks, and determine other ideological criteria.

Policies are anticipatory because they seek to guide future actions and decisions (Hudzik and Cordner, 1983). A policy assigns functions and delegates the authority to accomplish these functions to different units, positions, and individuals. The existence of formally articulated policy by the administrator identifies the role of the agency and sets the tone for behavior and procedures. The agency's style of correctional care, punishment, general behavior toward prisoners, and conduct of employees should be reflected in the policy.

Clearly written policies are vital to the agency to maintain organization control and to ensure compliance with a myriad of legal requirements.

To maintain legal operations, they should be based on and must reflect statutes and court holdings. Policies summarize and turn legislation, court decisions, executive orders or regulations into operational practices (Sechrest and Collins, 1989). Policy statements, either written or verbal, constitute the legal foundation for directing and controlling employees.

Since policy defines the chain of authority, it also defines the chain of liability. By their administrative function, administrators are responsible for seven basic management functions: planning, organizing, staffing, directing, coordinating, reporting, and budgeting (Gulick, 1937). Administrators fulfill many of these management functions through established policies by: (1) directing employees in the tasks of their jobs, (2) keeping employees abreast of legal and technological developments in the profession, (3) organizing an ongoing systematic process where goals and objectives of the organization are explained to employees, and (4) explaining to employees their responsibilities regarding implementation of the policies. At the implementation level, an agency establishes expectations and provides outcomes, which can be measured to evaluate if the agency is meeting its responsibilities to the public and inmates.

Policy statements set forth general guidelines for employees, which provide clear and distinct boundaries for individual discretion in decision making. In developing policies, the primary intent is not to totally eliminate an officer's discretion through a written policy. Rather, policies and procedures set discretionary limits for the decision maker, regardless of his or her level in the organization, instead of specifying the decisions to be made (Robbins, 1976).

Policies should not eliminate the use of discretion by the correctional officer, but rather structure and guide discretionary actions. Obviously, it is impractical to attempt to develop policies for every conceivable encounter or problem an officer may face. Therefore, guidance, direction, and structure must be formulated to direct an officer's course of action. The major objectives of administrative guidance may be described as controlling correctional officers' actions, providing guidance for individual officers, coordinating efforts by which to approach particular problems, and providing accountability of employees' actions and decision making.

While policies provide guides to officers' thinking, procedures provide officers with guides to action. Procedures describe the methods for performing an operation by outlining, in order, the steps that must be performed and the personnel responsible (American Correctional Association, 1991). Procedures provide a standing plan that spells out certain actions necessary to accomplish a task (Houston, 1995). Procedures differ from policies in that they direct action in a particular situation for employees to perform a specific task within the guidelines of policies. Policies provide the framework of guidance, while procedures describe a method of operation while allowing some flexibility for employee actions. Procedures anticipate actual occupational needs that will arise in the day-to-day management of an agency and provide employees with specific guidance. A policy document will contain both a broad policy statement and procedures outlining specific employee tasks and responsibilities.

When formulating policies, the five following recommendations should be kept in mind:

1. Policies and procedures should be written rather than oral. Written policies provide a permanent record to which employees always can refer.

2. Written guidance should be drafted carefully with words chosen deliberately. It should be compiled into a comprehensive manual.

3. Written guidance should give employees notice of what kinds of behaviors are acceptable and unacceptable to management. They assist in preventing improper conduct and satisfying legal requirements.

4. A regular review process should be mandatory. A system of regular review aids in ensuring attention to a particular problem. It is essential that correctional agencies be consistent and current with the status of the law. Competent legal counsel should review all policies.

5. Finally, some method of annual auditing of compliance and maintenance of records and policies is needed. This will assist in ensuring an annual review is being performed and help to keep policies current.

The first line of defense against potential litigation and proper employee conduct is well-written policies. In the area of use of force, policy can assist in reducing allegations of excessive force or brutality, reducing prospective civil lawsuits, improving employee decision making, and reducing the burden of liability on the part of the organization's administrators. To avoid liability, policies should be attentive to the four Cs. They should be current, comprehensive, consistent, and constitutional.

Use-of-force Policy Implementation

A persistent dilemma administrators face today is managing the proper use of force in the correctional facility. Correctional officers possess a privilege to use force in self-defense, in defense of others, to enforce prison rules and regulations, to prevent a crime, and to prevent escape. Correctional officers face a myriad of circumstances daily in which force decision making is required. Balancing the need to use force and determining the degree of force to use can be problematic. Implementation of a solid and reasoned policy and set of procedures on proper use of force is an important strategy for correctional administrators.

Of course, the policy must be designed carefully, supported with appropriate control tactics, and force equipment. There must be a comprehensive training program for new officers, regular inservice training for current officers, a comprehensive review process for use-of-force incidents, and disciplinary procedures to deal with misuse of force. Developing and implementing a use-of-force policy does not imply that managing use of force means relying solely on a promulgated policy. This is only the first step. It is pointless to have a well-structured policy if personnel do not know the policy or if the policy has not been properly implemented. A concerted effort by management is required to ensure the policy is understood and fully implemented.

Operationalizing the legal requirements and statements of a policy into functional procedures is known as policy implementation. This involves a systematic process whereby management takes the written, verbal, or presumed operative statements of upper management and applies them to specific circumstances. Pressman and Wildavsky (1973) define implementation as the ability to forge subsequent links in the causal chain so as to obtain the described results. They advocate simplicity as the key component in the implementation process, because the fewer the steps involved in implementing the policy, the fewer the opportunities for something to go wrong. Ripley and Franklin (1982) define policy implementation as what happens after laws are passed authorizing a policy, a benefit, or some kind of tangible output.

The successful implementation of policy and procedure on the use of force occurs in several stages. Failure to accomplish any one of the stages in the following discussion could affect the overall implementation process significantly. Policies and procedures will be implemented best if they are developed with the involvement of staff from all operational areas (Sechrest and Collins, 1989). When formulating and/or revising a use-of-force policy, administrators should consider the following model.

1. Formulate a Policy Team

The administrator is responsible for developing and revising policies and procedures. Involving agency personnel is the best approach to ensuring future cooperation, and this process increases the acceptance and successful implementation of policy by personnel. This strategy is very important as it promotes a sense of ownership of the work and energy invested. Personnel from a variety of positions and rank within the organization should be assigned to assist in the researching, writing, and implementing of the policy. Inclusion of personnel whose job it is to apply policy should be formally involved in the policy development. For use-of-force policies, this team should consist of in-house experts, including force control instructors, officers, supervisors, an attorney, a risk manager, and a physician. These members should be selected based on their knowledge of both the total organization and their specific assignments. Furthermore, members should be selected who are insightful, articulate, and willing to speak and offer input and criticism.

The extent of personnel involvement can range from active work such as writing draft policies and procedures to reacting to drafts written by the administrator. It is important that all team members provide substantive input in the creation of the policy and on critical evaluation of the drafts. A team leader should be selected and carefully plan the role of each team member to correspond with his or her skills, experience, job responsibilities, and interests.

If the team has been assigned to develop or totally revamp the policy, the size of the group will depend on the department's resources, characteristics of the agency, access to clerical assistance, and time members can be away from their normal duties. Larger agencies may have the luxury of having more personnel and resources to devote exclusively to the project. Conversely, smaller agencies may have to depend on a committee approach to accomplish the task and assign only a few individuals to the team. The administrator will need to assemble the team in light of the resources available to the department.

Additionally, agencies may experience expansion and growth to the extent that this process should be used for the creation and management of a large range of significant policy subjects. Where this is occurring, leadership may create multiple policy teams that operate across agency lines. Serving on a policy team is a significant professional growth experience for participating staff. Finally, under all circumstances, this is an excellent process to formalize for the management of all policy creation and development.

2. Develop a Work Plan

A work plan will insure the necessary work is completed by responsible team members and that the process keeps moving. Various sections of the policy should be assigned to team members. For example, one individual may research how pepper spray may or may not be used while two other individuals work on developing a force continuum.

A timetable for meetings and realistic deadlines for assignments should be developed. Time must be allotted to research work on the drafts, and the team should meet to exchange ideas, discuss problems, review the progress of the work, and review each team member's work. One or two individuals must be assigned to actually pull all the research and sections together to form the first draft.

The work plan should include an outline of the policy and procedures section headings and priorities assigned to team members. Priorities may include the following items:

1. Identifying the philosophy of the department on using force and focusing the direction of the policy toward that philosophy

2. Reviewing other correctional agencies' use-of-force policies

3. Reviewing the current status of case law relevant to the use of force

4. Reviewing state and professional standards on the use of force

5. Reviewing current physical control measures and types of restraints

6. Reviewing equipment and products that legally can be used to control prisoners

7. Conducting an analysis of resistance situations within the facility to determine the levels of force required and where the potential for abuse may occur

8. Designing a reporting and documentation system, based on the analysis of use-of-force situations

9. Developing a force continuum, based on the analysis of force and resistance situations

10. Determining when medical personnel will be summoned to assess prisoners involved in a use-of-force situation

The work plan should adhere to a timetable, so plan meetings and deadlines in a realistic manner, and remain aware that in correctional facilities, the unexpected may occur at any time. The team leader should document the process, keep complete records of the work, including meetings, assignments, drafts, and final copies of policies implemented. Documenting the process will be useful in evaluating the team's work, demonstrating a good faith effort to the courts and inspection agencies.

3. Structure Your Policy on Use of Force

The purpose of the policy should be articulated. This will help personnel understand the full scope of the policy and the philosophy of the department. Policy statements should describe what to do in a clear and concise manner. The policy should include a written statement about minimizing and avoiding excessive force. A statement to the effect that personnel "will only use necessary and reasonable force to bring an incident under control, while protecting the lives of the officer or others" is recommended. Policy statements should not leave room for personnel to

interpret the policy on their own and should be written so they are consistent with the department's philosophy on the subject matter.

Procedures should be written in sequential order. This provides personnel with a description of the procedural steps in the order that they are
to be accomplished. Recall that procedures are guides to action and
describe how to do something. Use-of-force procedures should specify
when certain types of control measures and equipment may be authorized and under what types of resistance situations. Procedures should be
written to promote consistency within the agency. Since it is impossible
to predict every situation in which force may be used, force procedures
not only should be framed within a context of the law, but within parameters of discretion allowing officers some flexibility when deciding a
course of action. This can be done by incorporating a force continuum
into the procedures.

Structuring a use-of-force policy should be approached from the perspective that using force involves a spectrum of force options, which
include officer presence and verbal control, less-than-lethal force control
measures, and lethal force. It is recommended that one policy should be
designed to guide officers' use-of-force actions. Approaching force from
this philosophy provides specific guidance to officers working in the
facility and those whose work includes carrying weapons. The use-of-
force policy should be developed to meet the normal requirements of
working in the correctional facility and should address using verbal dialog, restraints, chemical agents or pepper spray, physical control tactics,
and impact weapons. Issues of responding to disturbances, riots, or
extracting a prisoner from a cell should be addressed in separate policies.

Based on team participation and research from the work plan, the
use-of-force policy should be structured to include the following nine
elements:

1. A philosophy and purpose of the department's use-of-force
   rationale (a policy statement). This statement should describe
   the overall goal for using force in corrections and identify constitutional and state law, which guides the use of force.

2. Definitions, which clearly describe control, resistance, force, malicious and sadistic force, lethal force, and less-than-lethal force.

3. A description of force authorization categorizing the justifiable circumstances under which force may by be used legitimately. This section also should include a discussion of authorized and unauthorized weapons available for officers in use-of-force situations.

4. Description of the use-of-force procedures and the force continuum. This should be the heart of the policy. Failing to integrate a force continuum into the policy creates a gap between philosophy and actual practice. The continuum provides guidance in decision making, provides a clearer picture of case law on reasonable force, helps in structuring a report on a force incident, and enhances courtroom testimony when an officer is explaining the decision-making process involved in selecting a course of action.

   The force continuum should be divided into levels of prisoner resistance or behaviors and appropriate and reasonable force measures and equipment available to the officer to control the inmate. The force continuum should be designed on an escalation/de-escalation principle, which starts with verbal dialog, then authorizes physical control measures, the use of chemicals or pepper spray, restraints, and impact weapons. There should be a section describing the proper use of restraints, aerosols and decontamination methods, and proper use of impact weapons. And, a section should be devoted to describing the justification for lethal force.

5. The procedure should describe when an officer is to summon a supervisor onto the scene and set forth under what circumstances audiovisual equipment will be used.

6. The procedure should specify the medical requirements following a use-of-force incident. When a prisoner is sprayed with an aerosol, struck with an impact weapon, controlled with a neck restraint, exhibits signs of medical distress, or complains of injuries, medical attention should be required.

7. The procedure should stipulate the reporting requirements after a lethal or less-than-lethal use-of-force altercation. The procedure

should specify when the report is to be submitted and stipulate the supervisory review process.

8. The procedure should stipulate the protocol for investigating every incident where personnel used lethal and less-than-lethal force, restraints, impact weapons, and aerosols. A report must accompany the final outcome of the investigation.

9. Training and competency requirements of all control measures and force equipment should be set forth within the policy.

4. Draft the Policy

This stage involves all team members preparing their respective assignment from the work plan. The draft should parallel the structure of the policy described earlier. The team leader should assign deadlines for the drafts to be submitted so that other team members may evaluate each member's work. A meeting date should be scheduled whereby the entire policy team convenes to discuss the drafts.

5. Review and Revise the Policy

At a scheduled team meeting, drafts of each team member's assignment should be reviewed and discussed. Legal counsel on the team or outside the department should review all section assignments to ensure the information is consistent with constitutional and state law. It is important to realize that correctional departments' guidelines can be affected strongly by not only criminal law, but also, the law of civil rights, civil liability, and administrative law. As such, the reviewing attorney(s) should be selected based on their expertise in those areas. The need for legal review cannot be overemphasized. An expert in the use of force familiar with professional standards and control measures also should review the documents.

The team leader should direct all team members to revise their assignment based on feedback and discussion from the review session. The leader should set deadlines for submission of revisions and a date for a full team meeting. Informal meetings should be allowed if personnel are having difficulty with the recommended revisions. The team leader should document the revision process.

6. Assemble and Distribute the Policy

Once all sections have been revised, the team leader should assemble all the revised sections into one document. Once this has been accomplished, the policy should be distributed to the full team for their comments. If the policy is approved by the team, it should be forwarded to the top administrator for final approval and distribution.

7. Train Personnel in the Policy

Following all input and revisions previously discussed, the team should establish a timetable for implementation. A use-of-force policy is one of the most critical policies in corrections. Solely relying on distributing the final policy and only requiring that personnel read and sign a statement indicating they have received a copy is not training. All personnel whom the policy effects must receive training in the policy. The time period in which to conduct the training depends on how many persons and units are affected and logistical factors associated with implementation.

The team leader should schedule blocks of training in which the policy will be disseminated. Providing training in the policy ensures all personnel have received a copy, read it, been allowed to ask questions regarding proper implementation, and have been exposed thoroughly to the agency's philosophy about the use of force. All supervisors should receive training in the policy prior to full implementation. Training in the policy should be conducted prior to its being implemented. All employees should be tested on their knowledge of the contents, actions to take based on the policy, and requirements of the policy. Documentation of the training and test scores should be retained in each employee's personnel file.

Beyond providing training in the policy, the department should provide regular training in the physical skills and the equipment authorized for use in the policy. Successful implementation of a policy begins with a knowledge of the directive and continues with how to transfer procedures into the work situation. Therefore, to ensure effective policy implementation, training must be focused on force decision making; properly using physical control skills; competency in using force equipment, including restraints, impact weapons, and aerosols; documenting and reporting use of force; and knowing medical assessment requirements.

Documentation of this training also must be recorded in each employee's personnel file. It is essential that all personnel learn and understand the nature of such policies before they actually are implemented. This is one of the best methods to guarantee successful policy implementation. Implementing policy by this approach helps to illustrate management's commitment to administrative control and resolves issues associated with the department's liability where policies may be a focal point on allegations of failure to train, failure to supervise, failure to direct, and on negligently entrusting force equipment to employees.

Training in a use-of-force policy and in the necessary physical skills and equipment is not a one-time event. It is an ongoing process where inservice refresher training is required on a regular basis. Use-of-force training requires competency in the use of control measures, proper use of equipment, weapons, and decision making. Updates in changes in procedures, laws, and tactics must be provided regularly. New personnel must be trained fully and be competent in the policy and requisite physical skills.

8. Implement the Policy

When implementing a critical policy such as the use of force, the administrator also should consider the following recommendations:

Using a Force Report Form

To ensure employees are submitting and completing reports properly on the incidence of the use of force, a reporting system is recommended. The development of reporting documents is necessary to describe incidents involving force fully and promptly for necessary and meaningful analysis of incident rates, patterns, and trends. A standardized form outlining and detailing all the pertinent information of the force incident is recommended. A use-of-force log should be maintained to record all incidents of the use of force in the department. It should be kept in the shift supervisor's office. A quarterly report of the log should be submitted to the administrator, and ultimately should be included in the agency's annual report.

An injury report should be developed indicating the extent of injuries sustained during the incident. There should be a separate form for the employee to complete along with a separate form completed by medical personnel that reflects injuries sustained by the prisoner.

Using a Supervisory Incident Report Review System

Management should design a mechanism to assess and evaluate the report and incidence of the use of force. A supervisor should be designated to review each force report for its completeness and accuracy. The reviewer should determine whether the report needs revision, assess its adherence to policy, and determine whether an investigation is warranted. If an investigation is required, the supervisor then would turn the report over to the investigatory unit for further processing.

Instituting a Use-of-force Statistical Tracking System

The agency should adopt a system in which use-of-force incidents can be tracked. A shift supervisor or designee should formally report quarterly to the administrator the frequency and nature of force incidents; proper or improper uses of force; number of investigations regarding force incidents, if any; location of force incidents; a breakdown of the actual incidents and rates, according to the type of force used; nature of injuries; weapons used; prisoners' assaults on officers; incident rate per prisoner ratio; and applications of force between shifts. The tracking system can be used to monitor the proper implementation of policy and provide information for policy revision. The system also can serve as an early warning system which can provide information on violations of policy to target additional training and to institute the required disciplinary process.

Continuing Research

Ongoing research is essential in keeping policy current with what truly occurs within the department. Research assists in keeping policy current and training state of the art. Research in the use of force should be focused on prisoner resistance and assault situations, legal and liability issues, physical skills and equipment considerations, and methods of improving communication and training in conflict resolution.

Apply the Policy

Once written and implemented, the organization must ensure the policy is being followed by all personnel. Normally, this responsibility rests with first-line supervisors. The agency must ensure these supervisors are knowledgeable in all facets of the policy, can recognize proper use of force, can review force reports effectively, and can understand if the agency's disciplinary process policy is violated. If the policy is going to be operational, it must be enforced by supervisors. Beyond supervisors, internal investigation personnel may bear responsibility for ensuring that the policy is being followed.

9. Evaluate and Revise the Policy

No matter how well written, the policy will need periodic evaluation, review, and updates. Policies should be reviewed on an annual basis. The evaluation process determines whether the policy works and is being implemented properly. A simple test does not exist by which to assess the validity of the policy. The administrator must consider several factors when deciding the future direction of the policy. When evaluating policy, Carter (1986) recommends administrators should pose questions which address the following six criteria:

1. *Concept*—Was the subject matter that was addressed by the policy an important issue in correctional management? Was the subject matter conceptually sound and consistent with accepted principles of organization and administration?

2. *Structure*—Was the policy prepared in such a manner so that personnel can know what is prescribed and what is prohibited? Was the policy explicit and clear with respect to organizational expectations? Was the policy written in a manner that was easy to understand without conflict and duplication?

3. *Operations*—Does the policy seek and accomplish its intended results? Are the procedures easily and reasonably followed? Does the application of the policy ease or complicate the agency's activities? Is the policy still practical?

4. *Comprehension*—Did the policy address all issues and alternatives reasonably related to the subject matter? Did the policy provide guidance through its policy statement and procedures?

5. *Fundamental Fairness*—Did the policy treat all persons at issue—whether they were prisoners or agency employees—in an equitable, impartial, nondiscriminatory, ethical, and fundamentally fair manner?

6. *Jurisprudence*—Were the mandates of the policy consistent with the current status of the law? Did the policy adequately protect prisoners' rights? Did the policy adequately protect agency personnel and the agency from liability? Was the policy consistent with the principles of administrative law? Does the policy still comply with court decisions, constitutional requirements, and professional standards?

Those responsible for evaluating policy should use these assessment questions as guideposts to determine the utility of departmental policy. Being aware there is no magic formula for determining acceptability, administrators' experience and intuition can guide them in the evaluation process once these questions are answered. The next step is to determine the nature of the change, which must occur in the policy and recycle the policy through stage two, developing a work plan.

Conclusion

Developing, implementing, and revising a use-of-force policy is an important responsibility for the correctional administrator. It involves commitment, support from employees, and a willingness to enforce the policy once it is developed. Following the model presented in this chapter can assist the administrator in accomplishing a seemingly overwhelming task. The advantage to incorporating this model is that it provides a systematic structure when considering policy development or the revision process. These strategies provide administrative guidance to a selected team assigned to design the policy. It provides a process whereby policy development and implementation can be structured and documented. It ensures the organization's philosophy and objectives are clearly articulated. This process involves a team approach by using varying positions and ranks of personnel in the agency, thereby creating ownership in the process, and participation in decision making within the total organization. The model suggested also ensures legal and professional standards will be included in the policy, and it sets up a framework in which the policy can be implemented, evaluated, and revised effectively. This strategy illustrates a sound basis for effective supervision.

Obviously, policies and guidelines are not a panacea or a "quick fix" for the administrator or the agency. Astute administrators, however, should realize their responsibility and the court's legal concerns regarding the use of force in a correctional facility. Administrators must be committed to proper implementation, personnel training, and proper enforcement of the use-of-force policy. This adheres to fundamental administrative principles and at the same time enables administrators to lead their department effectively. If corrections is to become more effective in the future, administrators must create an environment that fosters a team effort and is grounded in a legitimate sound policy.

Conclusion

During 1997, a videotape of several correctional officers beating and abusing inmates in a Texas county jail was released to the news media. Observers were understandably shocked and horrified by what they saw on the videotape. Amid public outrage, the Texas Jail Standards Commission passed a rule that would require counties to draft formal use-of-force policies.

One commissioner complained that most sheriffs already had use-of-force policies and that this was just more paperwork. Another commission member said "Another written policy is not going to prevent something like this. More knowledge and training and mandatory training on the use of force would do more to prevent it than a file cabinet full of policies."

Conclusion

These responses typify the current debate surrounding use of force in corrections. Policies alone cannot prevent excessive use-of-force cases; at the same time, it is also true that use of force in corrections will continue—it is simply part of the job. Policies and training can provide correctional officers with clear standards of conduct so that they can conform their actions to these standards of conduct.

Clear and comprehensive policies, thorough, detailed training, and effective procedures for monitoring and reviewing use-of-force incidents can eliminate bad habits, correct mistaken assumptions, and show correctional officers how to do their jobs to the best of their ability. Everybody benefits from well-constructed use-of-force policies and training—officers know how to do their jobs better and know what is expected of them. Inmates are less likely to be victimized by overzealous, ill-informed officers, and correctional administrators are less likely to encounter expensive, embarrassing lawsuits alleging excessive use of force.

We have stressed the importance of training, but the reality is that many departments cannot afford it or cannot allow correctional officers to be away from work for extended periods of time. One solution is use-of-force videotaped scenario training (Brown, 1998). Another solution is to consider the cost of not providing training.

Excessive force claims frequently arise from circumstances in which the correctional officer was just trying to do his or her job, to protect inmates from each other, protect institution property, or in self-defense or defense of another officer. Correctional officers frequently work alone, without other officers nearby to either aid or observe them. Additionally, they are forced to make split-second decisions while dealing with a population that is often volatile and willing to use force. In these situations, most often, there are few witnesses other than the complaining inmate and the officer, and there is a substantial difference in their statements concerning what actually occurred.

A correctional officer is duty bound to do his or her job, including using force, when necessary. When force becomes "excessive" is a legal determination, based on whether the force was out of proportion to the need. Institutional policies, as well as court decisions and state and federal statutes, provide guidance for the correctional officer. Standards and legal language do not always provide guidance for every conceivable situation, however. Here, department training provides the understanding of the proper degree of force to use, as well as how to appropriately use force in any given situation.

This discussion highlights the importance of having a clear policy to guide use of force, the necessity of having good training to accomplish this policy, and the importance of thorough and fair review procedures to document and investigate complaints. With all of these present, excessive force claims will not be eliminated, but they will be reduced, and inmates are less likely to be successful, as they are less likely to be the victims of excessive force.

Changes in use-of-force policies are necessary as technology changes. A current example is the debate over the appropriate use of less-than-lethal weaponry. But the basic standard remains the same—reasonableness. This is a legal standard; thus, correctional officers must know how the courts define it. But correctional officers also must know their own institutional rules and policies, which often are formulated based on the law, and which provide greater guidance than generalized legal definitions.

Most professions, such as law and medicine, have adopted professional standards, and corrections is no exception. Core principles in corrections' code of ethics and standards for behavior include protection of self and others, maintenance of institution safety, and to do no harm to inmates (American Correctional Association, 1991). These ethical requirements may go beyond what minimal legal requirements do. This illustrates the difference between the letter of the law (what one must do to avoid liability) and the spirit of the law (what one "should" do).

Use of force is a common event, but one with serious consequences for all concerned. Improper use of force is a career-threatening situation, with high potential for both civil and criminal liability. Courts and the public often do not understand the world of the prison, and they have a hard time understanding the use of force. This is the reality that correctional officers and administrators must face. It makes a tough job tougher. But with education, clear guidance, and training, most problems can be avoided, and the officer and the department can be successful.

References

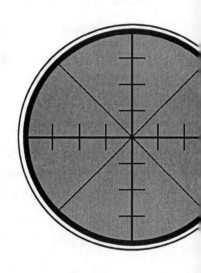

References

American Correctional Association. 1990. *Standards for Adult Correctional Institutions.* Lanham, Maryland: American Correctional Association.

———. 1991. *Guidelines for the Development of Policies and Procedures: Adult Correctional Institutions.* Lanham, Maryland: American Correctional Association.

Archambeault, W. C. and B. J. Archambeault. 1982. *Correctional Supervisory Management: Principles of Organization, Policy, and Law.* Englewood Cliffs, New Jersey: Prentice-Hall, Inc.

References

Atholl, J. 1954. *Shadow of the Gallows.* London: John Long.

Beccaria, C. B. (1963 [1764]). *On Crimes and Punishments.* New York: Bass-Merrill.

Bentham J. (1970 [1789]). An Introduction to the Principles of Morals and Legislation. In J. Burns and H. Hart, eds. *Collected Works.* London: Athlone Press.

Black, H. C. 1983. *Black's Law Dictionary,* Fifth edition. St. Paul, Minnesota: West Publishing.

Bowker, L. 1980. *Prison Victimization.* New York: Elsevier.

Brown, P. 1998. Scenario Use of Force Training: Low Cost, High Dividends. *Corrections Compendium.* 23(6): 4-5.

Camp, C. and George Camp. 1998. *Corrections Yearbook 1998.* Middletown, Connecticut: Criminal Justice Institute, Inc.

Carter, D. L. 1986. Explaining Policies and Procedures as a Function of Administrative Control. Paper presented at the annual meeting of the Academy of Criminal Justice Sciences, Orlando, Florida.

Certo, S. C. 1985. *Principles of Modern Management,* Third edition. Dubuque, Iowa: Wm. C. Brown.

Christian, T. F. 1999. *Conflict Management and Conflict Resolution in Corrections.* Lanham, Maryland: American Correctional Association.

Clear, T. and L. Cole. 1997. *American Corrections.* Belmont, California: Wadsworth.

Collins, W. C. 1997. *Correctional Law for the Correctional Officer,* Second edition. Lanham, Maryland: American Correctional Association.

Corrections Journal. 1998. Punitive Damages from Lawsuit Stun California State Officials. December 22.

The Corrections Professional. 1999. Use-of-force Rules Change in California. March.

del Carmen, R. V. 1991. *Civil Liabilities in American Policing: A Text for Law Enforcement Personnel.* Englewood Cliffs, New Jersey: Prentice-Hall, Inc.

————. 1992. The Supreme Court and Prison Excessive Use of Force Cases: Does One Test Fit All? *Federal Probation.* 56(2):44-47 (June).

Drapkin, M. 1996. *Developing Policies and Procedures for Jails.* Lanham, Maryland: American Correctional Association.

Ekland-Olson, S., D. Barrich, and L. Cohen. 1983. Prison Overcrowding and Disciplinary Problems: An Analysis of the Texas Prison System. *Journal of Applied Behavioral Science.* 19:2, 163-176.

Eulau, H. and K. Prewitt. 1973. Labyrinths of Democracy. In Charles O. Jones, ed. *An Introduction to the Study of Public Policy*, Second edition. North Scituate, Massachusetts: Duxbury Press.

Federal Bureau of Prisons. 1997. *Use of Force Policy.* Washington, D.C.: Federal Bureau of Prisons.

Gamire, B. 1985. *Local Government Police Management*, Second edition. Washington, D.C.: International City Management Association.

Gulick, L. 1937. *Papers on the Science of Administration.* New York: Institute of Public Administration.

Hansen, R., and H. Daley. 1995. *Challenging the Conditions of Prisons and Jails: A Report on Section 1983 Litigation.* Washington, D.C.: U.S. Department of Justice.

Hemmens, C. 1997. We're Doing the Best We Can: The Eighth Amendment, Health Care Delivery, and the Development of Professional Standards. *American Jails.* 11:4- 11.

Hemmens, C., and J. Marquart. 1998. Fear and Loathing in the Joint: The Impact of Race and Age on Inmate Support for Prison AIDS Policies. *The Prison Journal.* 78:2.

Houston, J. 1995. *Correctional Management.* Nelson-Hall: Chicago.

Hudzik, J, and G. Cordne. 1985. *Planning in Criminal Justice Organizations and Systems.* New York: Macmillan.

Human Rights Watch. 1997. *Cold Storage: Super-Maximum Security Confinement in Indiana.* New York: Human Rights Watch.

Inciardi, J. A. 1990. *Criminal Justice.* Orlando, Florida: Harcourt Brace Jovanovich.

Jacobs, J. 1977. *Stateville.* Chicago: University of Chicago Press.

Johnson, R. 1990. *Death Work: A Study of the Modern Execution Process.* Pacific Grove, California: Brooks-Cole.

Jones, M. and del Carmen, R. V. 1992. When Do Probation and Parole Officers Enjoy the Same Immunity As Judges? *Federal Probation.* 56: 36-41.

Kant, I. 1965 [1787]). *Critique of Pure Reason.* New York: St. Martin's Press.

Keve, P. 1991. *Prisons and the American Conscience: A History of U.S. Federal Corrections.* Carbondale, Illinois: Southern Illinois University Press.

———. 1996. *Measuring Excellence: the History of Correctional Standards and Accreditation.* Lanham, Maryland: American Correctional Association.

Kratcoski, P. 1987. The Implications of Research Explaining Prison Violence and Disruption. *Federal Probation.* 52, 27-32.

Light, S. 1991. Assaults on Prison Officers: Interactional Themes. *Justice Quarterly.* 8:2, 243-261.

Locke, J. (1980 [1690]). *Second Treatise of Civil Government.* Indianapolis, Indiana: Hackett.

Lombardo, L. 1982. *Guards Imprisoned.* New York: Elsevier.

Maahs, J. and R. del Carmen. 1995. Curtailing Section 1983 Inmate Litigation: Laws, Practices, and Proposals. *Federal Probation*. 59, 53-61.

Marquart, J. W. 1986. Prison Guards and the Use of Physical Coercion as a Mechanism of Social Control. *Criminology*. 24, 347-366.

Marquart, J. W., S. Ekland-Olson, and J. R. Sorensen. 1994. *The Rope, the Chair, and the Needle*. Austin, Texas: University of Texas Press.

Miller, N. 1995. Less-Than-Lethal Force Weaponry: Law Enforcement and Correctional Agency Civil Law Liability for the Use of Excessive Force. *Creighton Law Review*. 28: 733-794.

Morris, N., and D. Rothman. 1995. *The Oxford History of the Prison: The Practice of Punishment in Western Society*. New York: Oxford University Press.

Morris, T. and P. Morris. 1980. Where Staff and Prisoners Meet. In B. Crouch, ed. *The Keepers: Prison Guards and Contemporary Corrections*. Springfield, Illinois: Charles C. Thomas.

Newman, G. 1985. *The Punishment Response*. Albany, New York: Harrow and Heston.

Palmer, J. 1997. *Constitutional Rights of Prisoners*. Cincinnati, Ohio: Anderson Publishing.

Pressman, J. L. and A. B. Wildavsky. 1973. *Implementation*. Berkley, California: University of California Press.

Radzinowicz, L. 1948. *A History of English Common Law*. New York: Macmillan.

Ripley, R. B. and G. A. Franklin. 1982. *Bureaucracy and Policy Implementation*. Homewood, Illinois: The Dorsey Press.

Robbins, S. 1976. *The Administration Process*. Englewood Cliffs, New Jersey: Prentice-Hall.

Roberts, J. W. 1997. *Reform and Retribution: An Illustrated History of American Prisons*. Lanham, Maryland: American Correctional Association.

Ross, D. L. 1997. Emerging Trends in Correctional Civil Liability Cases: A Content Analysis of Federal Court Decisions of Title 42 United States Code Section 1983: 1970 to 1994. *Journal of Criminal Justice*. 25, (6):501-515.

Rothman, David J. 1971. *The Discovery of the Asylum*. New York: Harper Collins.

Rotman, E. 1995. The Failure of Reform: United States, 1865-1965. In N. Morris and D. Rothman, eds. *The Oxford History of the Prison*. New York: Oxford.

Rowan, J. R. 1996. Who is Safer in Male Maximum Security Prisons? *Corrections Today*. 58:2.

Sechrest, D. K. and W. C. Collins. 1989. *Jail Management and Liability Issues*. Olympia, Washington: Coral Gables Publishing.

Sieh, E. 1989. The Principle of Lease Eligibility. *Criminal Justice Policy Review*. 3:1.

Staples, W. G. 1990. *Castles of Our Conscience: Social Control and the American State, 1800-1985*. New Brunswick, New Jersey: Rutgers University Press.

Stephan, J. 1997. *Census of State and Federal Correctional Facilities, 1995*. Washington, D.C.: United States Department of Justice.

Toch, H. 1977. *Living in Prison: The Ecology of Survival*. New York: Free Press.

Walker, J. 1996. Police and Correctional Use of Force: Legal and Policy Standards and Implications. *Crime and Delinquency*. 42:1, 144-156.

Weber, M. 1947. *The Theory of Social and Economic Organization*. New York: The Free Press.

Significant Supreme Court Decisions

Bell v. Wollfish, 441 U.S. 520 (1979)

Coffin v. Reichard, 143 F.2d 443 (6th Cir., 1944)

Cooper v. Pate, 378 U.S. 546 (1964)

Estelle v. Gamble, 429 U.S. 97 (1976)

Ex parte Hull, 312 U.S. 546 (1941)

Farmer v. Brennan, 511 U.S. 825 (1994)

Garner v. Tennessee, 471 U.S. 1 (1985)

Giroux v. Sherman (807 F. Supp. 1182, E.D. PA. 1992)

Hewitt v. Helms, 459 U.S. 460 (1983)

Holt v. Sarver, 309 F.Supp. 362 (E.D. Ark. 1970, aff'd 442 F.2d 304)

Hudson v. McMillan, 503 U.S. 1 (1992)

Monell v. Department of Social Services of the City of New York, 436 U.S. 658 (1978)

Monroe v. Pape, 365 U.S. 167 (1961)

O'Lone v. Estate of Shabazz, 482 U.S. 342 (1987)

Richardson v. McKnight, 117 S. Ct. 2100 (1997)

Rhodes v. Chapman, 454 U.S. 337 (1981)

Ruffin v. Commonwealth, 62 Va. (21 Gratt.) 790 (1871)

Vineyard v. County of Murray, Georgia, 990 F.2d 1207 (1983)

Whitley v. Albers, 475 U.S. 312 (1986)

Wilson v. Seiter, 501 U.S. 294 (1991)

Wolff v. McDonald, 418 U.S. 539 (1974)

Appendix A

ACA Standards on Use of Force

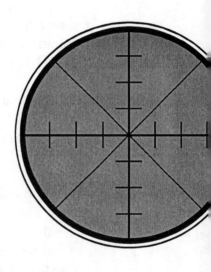

The American Correctional Association has been among the leaders in the development of standards for the corrections profession. Included among these are standards regarding the use of force in corrections. A number of state corrections departments either have incorporated portions of these standards, or make reference to them in their policies. A copy of the ACA Standards regarding use of force in corrections is provided. The standards are from the manuals for *Adult Correctional Institutions* and *Adult Local Detention Facilities*, (ALDF) both third editions.

3-4087   All security and custody personnel are trained in approved methods of self-defense and the use of force as a last resort to control inmates.
(Also 3-ALDF-1D-17)

3-4088   Written policy, procedure, and practice provide that all personnel authorized to use firearms receive appropriate training before being assigned to a post involving the possible use of such weapons. Firearms training covers the use, safety, and care of firearms and the constraints on their use. All personnel authorized to use firearms must demonstrate competency in their use at least annually.
(Also 3-ALDF-1D-18)

3-4089   All personnel authorized to use chemical agents receive thorough training in their use and in the treatment of individuals exposed to a chemical agent.
(Also 3-ALDF-1D-19)

3-4183-1   Written policy, procedure, and practice provide that when an offender is placed in a four/five-point restraint (arms, head and legs secured), advance approval must be obtained from the warden/superintendent or designee. Subsequently, the health authority or designee must be notified to assess the inmate's medical and mental health condition, and to advise whether, on the basis of serious danger to self or others, the inmate should be placed in a medical/mental health unit for emergency involuntary treatment with sedation and/or other medical management, as appropriate. If the offender is not transferred to a medical/mental health unit and is restrained in a four/five-point position, the following minimum procedures will be followed:

1. Direct visual observation by staff must be continuous prior to obtaining approval from the health authority or designee;

2. Subsequent visual observation must be made at least every 15 minutes; and,

3. Restraint procedures are in accordance with guidelines endorsed by the designated health authority.

(Also 3-ALDF 3A-17-1)

3-4191   Written policy and procedure govern the availability, control, and use of chemical agents, electrical disablers, and related security devices and specify the level of authority required for their access and use. Chemical agents and electrical disablers are used only with the authorization of the warden/superintendent or designee.

(Also 3-ALDF-3A-25)

3-4192   Written policy, procedure, and practice provide that the institution maintains a written record of routine and emergency distributions of security equipment.

(Also 3-ALDF-3A-26)

3-4193   Firearms, chemical agents, and related security equipment are inventoried at least monthly to determine their condition and expiration dates.

(Also 3-ALDF-3A-27)

3-4194   Written policy, procedure, and practice provide that written reports are submitted to the warden/superintendent or designee no later than the conclusion of the tour of duty when any of the following occur:

—discharge of a firearm or other weapon

—use of chemical agents to control inmates

—use of force to control inmates

—inmate(s) remain in restraints at the end of the shift

(Also 3-ALDF-3A-28)

3-4195   Written policy, procedure, and practice provide that all persons injured in an incident receive immediate medical examination and treatment.
(Also 3-ALDF-3A-29)

3-4196   Written policy and procedure govern the use of firearms, including the following:

    1. Weapons are subjected to stringent safety regulations and inspections.

    2. Except in emergency situations, employees carrying firearms are assigned only to watchtowers, gun walks, mobile patrols, or other positions that are inaccessible to inmates.

    3. Employees supervising inmates outside the institution's perimeter follow specific procedures for ensuring the security of the weapons.

    4. Employees are instructed to use deadly force only after other actions have been tried and found inffective, unless the employee believes that a person's life is immediately threatened.

(Also 3-ALDF-3A-32)

3-4197   Written policy, procedure, and practice provide for safe unloading and reloading of firearms.
(Also 3-ALDF-3A-30)

3-4198   Written policy, procedure, and practice restrict the use of physical force to instances of justifiable self-defense, protection of others, protection of property, and prevention of escapes, and then only as a last resort and in accordance with appropriate statutory authority. In no event is physical force justifiable as punishment. A written report is prepared following all uses of force and is submitted to administrative staff for review.
(Also 3-ALDF-3A-31)

Appendix B
Sample Policies on Use of Force from Connecticut, Florida, Montana, and the Federal Bureau of Prisons

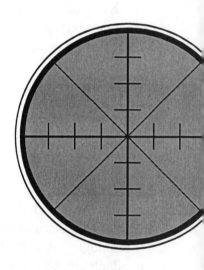

As the survey results in Chapter 4 indicate, there is substantial variety in use-of-force policies and procedures among corrections departments. Departments vary in terms of issues covered and depth of coverage of issues. What constitutes a "good" policy is subject to debate. In Chapter 5, we discussed the common topics included in use-of-force policies, and in Chapter 6, we discussed how to develop a sound policy and how to effectively implement such a policy.

Included here are sample use-of-force policies, from Connecticut (effective as of 1998), Florida (effective as of 1998), Montana (effective as of 1987), and the Federal Bureau of Prisons (effective as of 1996). All are used by permission of the respective departments. These polices were selected for inclusion here for several reasons. First, we wanted to include polices from departments in different regions of the country. Florida is from the South, Connecticut from the Northeast, and Montana from the West. The Federal Bureau of Prisons covers the entire country. Second, we wanted to include polices from departments of different sizes. Montana is a relatively small department, Connecticut is middle-sized, and Florida is a large department. The Federal Bureau of Prisons, of course, is the largest corrections department of all. Third, and most importantly, we wanted to include polices which discuss different issues in varying degrees.

Each of these polices is reproduced below in its entirety, so that the reader may compare them for style, length, topics covered, and degree of coverage. A few comments about each of these policies is in order, however.

Connecticut

Connecticut's use-of-force policy comes in the form of an "administrative directive," and is just six pages in length. There is a very short statement of policy, followed by citations to authority, including state statutes, and the American Correctional Association standards. A list of definitions of terms is included. This is followed by an enumeration of general principles and a discussion of the various types of use-of-force techniques and technologies. A brief discussion of procedures for reporting use-of-force incidents is included. Finally, two sample forms are attached. The Connecticut policy is relatively brief, compared to other polices. It is, however, clearly written and provides reference to other authorities.

Florida

Florida's use-of-force policy is quite detailed. It consists of more than twenty pages. It includes a comprehensive definition of the use of force and detailed procedures for filling out use-of-force incident reports. A discussion of various use-of-force devices and techniques is included, as well. Particular attention is paid to firearms, electronic devices, and chemical agents.

Montana

Montana's use-of-force policy does not cite other standards for authority, instead relying on state statutes. The policy is twelve pages in length, and includes a number of definitions, as well as a general statement of policy regarding use of force. Also included is a detailed discussion of the use-of-force continuum and the varying levels of use of force. There is little attention paid to reporting procedures, however. Specialized use-of-force techniques and technologies are dealt with in separate attachments, and these provide clear information and instruction.

Federal Bureau of Prisons

The Federal Bureau of Prisons use-of-force policy is relatively long and quite detailed. It combines rules with information on how to implement the rules, in an easy to understand format. There is a great deal of reference to standards. Objectives and principles are clearly stated. There are sections on specific types of force, and on how to avoid the use of force. Attached are a number of reporting forms. These are, by far, the most detailed and complex of the selected departments.

All of these sample policies have their pluses and minuses. They are included here to provide the reader with an opportunity to compare different approaches to the situation.

State of Connecticut

Department of Corrections
Administrative Directive
Directive Number: 6.5
Effective Date: August 3, 1998
Supersedes: Use of Force—1/25/93
Approved By: (initialed and dated)
Title: Use of Force

1. <u>Policy</u>. Use of physical force shall be authorized only when reasonably necessary to protect any person, prevent escape, prevent damage to property, or maintain order and discipline. The level of physical force shall be minimal, incremental and appropriate to the immediate circumstances.

2. <u>Authority and Reference</u>.

   A. Connecticut General Statutes Section 18-81, 53a-18, 53a-19, 53a- 20, 53a-21 and 53a-22.

   B. American Correctional Association, Standards for Adult Probation and Parole Field Services, Second Edition, March 1981, Standards 2-3158 and 2-3159.

   C. American Correctional Association, Standards for Adult Correctional Institutions, Third Edition, January 1990, Standards 3-4087, 3-4183, 3-4194, 3-4196, 3-4198 and 3-4268.

   D. American Correctional Association, Standards for Adult Local Detention Facilities, Third Edition, March 1991, Standards 3-ALDF-1D-17, 3-ALDF-3A-17, 3-ALDF-3A-28, 3-ALDF-3A-29, 3-ALDF-3A-31, and 3-ALDF-3E-O8.

E. Administrative Directives 2.7, Training and Staff
    Development; 6.4, Transportation and Community
    Supervision of Inmates; 6.6, Reporting of Incidents; 6.9,
    Control of Contraband and Physical Evidence; 7.2,
    Armories; 7.4, Emergency Response Units; and 9.4,
    Restrictive Housing.

3. <u>Definitions</u>. For the purposes stated herein, the following
    definitions apply:

    A. <u>Chemical Agent Devices</u>. Chemical agent devices consist of
        two (2) categories: (1) Category I devices are hand held
        aerosol dispensers and (2) Category II devices consist of all
        methods of administration other then hand held aerosol devices.

    B. <u>Deadly Physical Force</u>. Force which may reasonably be
        expected to cause death or serious injury.

    C. <u>Force</u>. Physical contact or contact through use of an armory
        item by a staff member in a confrontational situation to
        establish control or restore order.

    D. <u>Full Stationary Restraint</u>. Securing an inmate by the four (4)
        points of the arms and legs to a stationary horizontal surface
        or device, restricting the inmate's movement.

    E. <u>In-Cell Restraint</u>. Restraint within a cell of an acutely
        disruptive inmate utilizing one or more of the following
        restraining devices as appropriate: soft restraints, handcuffs,
        leg irons, bellychains, flex cuffs and/or black box.

    F. <u>Non-Deadly Physical Force</u>. Physical force not intended nor
        reasonably expected to cause death or serious injury.

    G. <u>Lethal Ammunition</u>. Ammunition that when used may
        reasonably be expected to cause death or serious injury.

    H. <u>Non-Lethal Ammunition</u>. Ammunition, to include Category
        II chemical agent projectiles, not reasonably expected to
        cause death or serious injury.

4. <u>General Principles</u>.

   A. Confrontation shall be deferred when such physical force is likely to result in escalation of the incident.

   B. Whenever possible, control and compliance shall be achieved by verbal intervention, defusing tension, warning, reprimand, direct order, disciplinary action. Physical force shall normally be the course of last resort.

   C. Physical force shall only be used to the degree and duration necessary to achieve its authorized objective.

   D. Physical force shall not be used for the harassment or punishment of any person.

   E. Use of physical force may be carried out by personnel in hazardous duty classifications. Use of physical force by other personnel shall be used in accordance with Section 16 of this Directive.

   F. An employee issued an armory item shall be authorized to use the item subject to the chain of command and in accordance with this Directive.

   G. Prior to the use of deadly physical force a verbal warning shall be used to the extent feasible.

   H. This Directive shall be subject to the provisions of related Administrative Directives (e.g., 2.7, Training and Staff Development; 6.4, Transportation and Community Supervision of Inmates; 6.6, Reporting of Incidents; 7.2, Armories; 7.4, Emergency Response Units; and 9.4, Restrictive Housing).

5. <u>Use of Non-Deadly Physical Force</u>.

   A. <u>Protection of Persons</u>. Non-deadly physical force may be used to protect a person from an immediate physical threat.

   B. <u>Prevention of Escapes</u>. Non-deadly physical force may be used to prevent an inmate from escaping from custody.

C. Prevention of Property Damage. Non-deadly physical force may be used to prevent destruction of property.

D. Maintaining Order and Discipline. Non-deadly physical force may be used to enforce an order only when failure to comply with the order jeopardizes the safety of an individual or seriously threatens the security and control of the area. Such force shall be authorized and observed by a supervisor whenever possible.

6. Use of Deadly Physical Force. Deadly physical force shall be authorized for use only in accordance with this Section.

A. Protection of Persons. Deadly physical force may be used to defend any person from the use or imminent use of deadly physical force.

B. Prevention of Escapes. Deadly physical force may be used to prevent the escape from custody of an inmate when: (1) an employee reasonably believes the inmate has committed or attempted to commit a felony which involves the infliction or threatened infliction of serious physical injury upon another person; and (2) if, where feasible, the employee has given warning of intent to use deadly physical force.

7. Chemical Agents.

A. Category I Chemical Agents. A properly trained and currently certified custody supervisor, designated Community Services staff member, designated Security Division staff member and Central Transportation staff member may be authorized to routinely carry and use as appropriate a Category I chemical agent. Oleoresin Capsicum (OC) shall be authorized for use as appropriate during transportation in accordance with this Directive. A custody supervisor may authorize the issuance and use as appropriate of Category I chemical agents to trained and certified staff in accordance with this Directive. Upon the direction of a supervisor, a tactical operations

team member shall be authorized to carry and use Category
I chemical agents in accordance with this Directive.

B. Category II Chemical Agents. Specially trained and designated
staff may use Category II chemical agents on the authorization
of the highest ranking onsite facility supervisor and subject to
the direct supervision of a custody supervisor in accordance
with this Directive.

C. Decision Factors. The decision to utilize chemical agents
should consider among other factors: (1) immediate danger
posed by the inmate (e.g., active aggression, presence of
weapons, known history of assaultive behavior); (2) potential
injury to staff and/or inmate; (3) area where agent shall be
employed; (4) potential exposure or impact on uninvolved
persons; or (5) presence of known physical conditions
which may contraindicate use, (e.g., heart or respiratory
condition).

D. Decontamination. Decontamination of any exposed person and
the contaminated area shall be accomplished immediately
upon restoration of control. Protective equipment shall be
utilized. Personal decontamination shall include at a minimum:
(1) flushing of the eyes; (2) a shower and change of clothing;
(3) medical attention; and (4) removal of the person from
the effected area if possible.

8. Restraints.

A. Authorized Use. Restraints as a use of physical force may
be authorized: (1) to prevent escape; (2) to prevent injury to
others or self; (3) to prevent property damage; and (4) to
ensure compliance with an order. An inmate placed in
restraints for a period longer than one (1) hour shall be
placed on restrictive status in accordance with Administrative
Directive 9.4, Restrictive Housing. Use of restraints in
accordance with Administrative Directives 6.4,
Transportation and Community Supervision of Inmates, 9.4,

Restrictive Housing, or for routine movement shall not be considered a use of physical force under this Directive.

B. In-Cell Restraints. Use of in-cell restraints shall be in accordance with Administrative Directive 9.4, Restrictive Housing.

C. Full Stationary Restraints. Use of full stationary restraints for any purpose other than medical shall be in accordance with this Directive. Placement of an inmate in full stationary restraints on a restrictive housing status shall be authorized by the shift supervisor with the notification of the Unit Administrator within one (1) hour of placement. The Shift Supervisor shall review for release from restraints every two (2) hours. Staff shall observe the inmate, at a minimum, of every 15 minutes or continuously if medically required. Medical observation shall be every two (2) hours and shall include the temporary relaxing of restraints if medically indicated to ensure proper circulation. The facility administrator shall review the inmate's status every eight (8) hours and shall notify the appropriate Complex Warden if the restraint status continues beyond 24 hours.

An inmate shall be left in appropriate clothing and shall not be left unclothed. Adequate accommodations shall be made to relieve an inmate of necessary bodily functions.

Normally, four (4) point restraints shall be soft, wide and flexible. However, in the event that an inmate compromises the soft restraints, metal mechanical restrains may be used. The use of metal restraints for full stationary restraint shall be with the permission of the Unit Administrator, and shall require a supplemental incident report, in accordance with Administrative Directive 6.6, Reporting of Incidents.

Any devise used for full stationary restraint of an inmate shall require prior written authorization from the Commissioner or designee.

    D.   <u>Restricted Use</u>. Body bags, wet sheet packs and straight jackets shall not be allowed for use as a use of physical force.

9.   <u>Firearms</u>. Use of firearms with lethal ammunition may be used as authorized in accordance with Section 6. Use of firearms with non-lethal ammunition may be used in accordance with Sections 5(A), (B) and (C). Warning shots shall not be authorized. A round may be fired into the ground within the boundary of a correctional facility for effect to terminate potentially lethal inmate action. A firearm shall not be used if discharging it could reasonably be expected to endanger the life of any innocent bystander.

10. <u>Baton</u>. A PR-24 or strait baton may only be used by a current, trained tactical operations team member as directed by the Director of Security and shall be in accordance with Sections 5 and 6.

11. <u>Shield</u>. A shield may be authorized by a shift supervisor in accordance with Section 5.

12. <u>Medical Examination</u>. Medical evaluation and treatment shall be provided as soon as possible after the use of physical force and as appropriate.

13. <u>Video Recording</u>. A planned use of physical force within an institution shall be videotaped by a trained operator. The camera operator shall state identity of the operator, date, time, and location of the recording. The camera shall be continuously operated and focus on the central point of action avoiding any obstruction of view. Any break in the video recording of the incident shall require reintroduction of the recorder, date, time, location, and reason for and duration of the break in recording. Any movement within the facility of the inmate in conjunction with and directly related to the use of force incident shall also be video taped.

The videotape shall be properly labeled to include the institution, location, date, time, subject of the tape, and identity of the operator. The original tape shall be properly secured and maintained for a minimum of two years. The original tape shall be considered physical evidence in accordance with Administrative Directive 6.9, Control of Contraband and Physical Evidence. Any movement or relocation of the original tape shall be authorized by the Unit Administrator. The original tape shall be numbered as #1 and copies shall be sequentially numbered. All tapes shall be properly accounted for.

14. Reporting and Record Keeping. Whenever physical force is used a Use of Force Report CN 6501, Attachment A, shall be completed by each employee involved in or observing the use of force incident. This requirement shall not apply to the routine use of restraints which is not considered a use of physical force. In addition to a Use of Force Report CN 6501, a Use of Chemical Agents Report CN 6502, Attachment B, shall be completed for any circumstance where chemical agents are deployed. These reports shall be attached to the Incident Report and submitted as required in Administrative Directive 6.6, Reporting of Incidents.

15. Serious Incident Review. A Serious Incident Review shall be used to assess the appropriateness of a use of physical force in an incident.

   A. Circumstances. A Serious Incident Review shall be conducted whenever: (1) a firearm is discharged; (2) Category II chemical agents are used; and/or (3) a firearm is drawn in a community setting.

   B. Review Committee. A Serious Incident Review Committee shall be appointed within five (5) business days of the incident by the appropriate Deputy Commissioner/designee whose unit was involved in the incident. The committee shall consist of three (3) persons of managerial rank. The Chair shall be of the rank of Captain, Correctional Counselor Supervisor or above. No member of the review committee shall be from the unit where the incident took place.

C. <u>Committee Activities and Report</u>. The committee shall review and analyze all reports, examine any physical evidence and may interview any witnesses or participants. The committee shall issue a report describing: (1) whether the action taken was consistent with Department directives; (2) whether other, less severe means of physical force were available to resolve or prevent the incident; (3) what action should be taken to avoid such future incidents; and (4) any recommended changes in Department or unit directives. The committee's final report shall be prepared within 30 days of the incident.

D. <u>Report Review</u>. The report shall be submitted to the Unit Administrator for review. Within 10 business days of receiving the report the Unit Administrator shall forward the report with comments and recommendations to the appropriate Deputy Commissioner through the chain of command. Within five (5) business days the Deputy Commissioner shall forward the report and supporting documentation with comments and action taken to the Commissioner. Upon final disposition the report shall be maintained by the Commissioner/designee.

16. <u>Emergency Circumstances</u>. Nothing in this Directive shall prevent the highest ranking custody supervisor from taking immediate, reasonable action when circumstances require. Nothing in this Directive shall prevent an employee from taking immediate, reasonable action to protect self or others.

17. <u>Exceptions</u>. Any exception to the procedures in this Administrative Directive shall require prior written approval from the Commissioner.

CN 6501
10/29/92

Attachment A
USE OF FORCE REPORT

Individual _____ Summary_____

Unit _____ Report No. _____ Report Date _____

Prepared by _____ Title _____

Inmate Name _____ Inmate Number _____

Date, time and location of Incident _____

Circumstances leading to use of force _____
_____
_____
_____
_____
_____

Type and extent of force used (to include any armory items used)
_____
_____
_____
_____
_____
_____

Complete (only when appropriate) by staff member if assaulted by inmate: Do you feel that the inmate should be considered for criminal prosecution?

YES _____ NO _____

Staff Signature   Title   Date

Investigating Supervisor Signature   Title   Date

CN 6502
10/29/92

Attachment B
USE OF CHEMICAL AGENTS REPORT

Individual _____ Summary _____

Unit _____ Report No. _____ Report Date _____

Prepared by _____ Title _____

Issued to _____ Date/time issued _____

Issued by _____ Date/time returned _____

Date, time and location of Incident _____

Reason for use of chemical agent _____

_____

_____

_____

Supervisor authorizing use _____

Name/Title _____

Type(s) of chemical agent used and to what extent _____

_____

Date/time used _____

Used by (Name and Title) _____

Who was agent(s) used on _____

_____

_____
Staff Signature   Title   Date

_____
Investigating Supervisor Signature   Title   Date

142

State of Florida

Use of Force

I. General

   A. Employees are authorized to apply physical force on an inmate only when and to the degree that it reasonably appears necessary in order:

     1. To defend himself or another against an inmate using unlawful force;

     2. To prevent the escape from a state correctional institution of an inmate;

     3. To prevent the escape of an inmate during transporting or while outside of a correctional institution;

     4. To prevent damage to property;

     5. To quell a disturbance;

     6. To overcome physical resistance to a lawful command; or

     7. To restrain the inmate when ordered by a physician or designee in order to allow medical staff to administer medical treatment in accordance with the provisions of Section V of this chapter.

   B. Physical force shall be employed only as a last resort when it reasonably appears that other alternatives are not feasible. When the use of force is justified, only that amount and type of force that reasonably appears necessary to accomplish the authorized objective shall be employed.

   C. There shall be no corporal punishment of any kind. Handcuffs, leg irons, and other such devices shall be used only for restraint and not for punishment.

   D. The Superintendent shall ensure that an IOP regarding the provisions of this Chapter be established and be adhered to.

E. The provisions of this chapter shall be incorporated into the Florida Department of Corrections' Use of Force training curriculum.

II. Authorization for Use of Force Report

Whenever possible, authorization to use physical force should be obtained prior to its use. Where there is time and circumstances permit, the highest ranking individual available should be consulted prior to using force. Whenever force is authorized, the employee who was responsible for making the decision to have force applied shall prepare, date, and sign the Authorization for Use of Force Report (DC3-320), indicating why force was ordered.

III. Report of Force Used

A. Whenever force is used, a detailed written "Report of Force Used" (DC3-300) shall be prepared, dated, and signed by each employee using force. Blanket or generic reports are not sufficient.

IV. Preparation of Use of Force Report

The person who actually participates in Use of Force shall complete the Authorization for Use of Force or the Use of Force Report either during or immediately after the tour of duty in which the authorization of force or application of force occurred, but prior to the employee's normal days off, an official holiday, or the taking of annual leave by the employee. If any emergency arises, the Superintendent may authorize the employee to complete the report immediately upon his return to his duty station. The report must be submitted to the Superintendent no later than five (5) working days after the incident.

Use of Force Reports are to be completed by each employee who actually applied the force. Use of Force Reports shall be prepared and different entries made on this form at different stages of the proceeding as set forth in this section.

A. Heading

This section should be self-explanatory. It will include inmate's name, number, institution, and date.

B. Section I

1. Report of Person Using Force—Statement of Facts

Clearly and concisely state fully the exact circumstances leading to the Use of Force (i.e., who, what, when, where, how, and why) and your part in the Use of Force. When referring to time of occurrence, use Standard Time or daylight savings time when appropriate, with A.M. or P.M. following. Each employee involved is responsible for individual preparation of this section based on what the employee did during the situation.

2. Type and Amount of Force Used

Describe in detail the type and amount of force used and the action of each employee involved in the incident. It is not sufficient to simply state "only minimum force was used."

C. Section II

1. Report of Investigation

A complete and thorough investigation will be conducted by designated staff with the findings fully stated. Each of the persons involved including the inmate is to be interviewed, as well as witnesses, if any, and the information obtained incorporated into the findings along with any other pertinent facts.

D. Section III is for the Superintendent's review and is self-explanatory. To be approved, the completed report must leave no doubt that force was indeed necessary and that only the amount of force necessary to control the individual situation was used.

E. Section IV is for the Regional Director's review. The Regional Director may request further investigation be made if his evaluation of the report would so indicate. The Regional Director will approve the report if he feels the type and amount of force was justified or will disapprove the Use of Force Report if he feels that the type and amount was not justified.

F. Distribution of the Use of Force Report will be according to the instructions on the form.

V. Use of Force to Administer Medical Treatment

Force or restraint may be used when ordered by a physician or designee in order to allow medical staff to administer medical treatment deemed essential. This force and/or restraint must be under the supervision of a physician or designee, and only when treatment is necessary to protect the health of other persons, as in the case of contagious and venereal diseases, or when treatment is offered in satisfaction of a duty to protect the inmate against self-inflicted injury or death. The physician shall prepare a report documenting the facts and reasons upon which the decision was based. The physician's report shall be attached to the employee's completed Report of Force Form.

VI. Report of Suspected Inmate Abuse

The objective is for staff to immediately report alleged violations to the appropriate authority.

Each employee who witnesses, or has reasonable cause to suspect, that an inmate has been unlawfully abused shall immediately prepare, date, and sign an "Independent Report" pursuant to s. 944.35(5) F.S., specifically describing the nature of the force used, the location and time of the incident, and the persons involved. The "Independent Report" may be a memo, letter, incident report, or any other form of written communication detailing the suspected unlawful abuse of force. It should be pointed out that the "Independent Report" should not be prepared on the "Use of Force Report" (Form DC 3-300). The independent report shall be delivered to the Inspector General of the department with a copy to be delivered to the Superintendent of the institution. The Inspector General shall immediately conduct an appropriate investigation and, if probable cause is determined that a violation of law has occurred, the respective State Attorney in the circuit in which the institution is located shall be notified.

VII. Penalties

A. "Any employee required to submit a Use of Force Report, who knowingly or willfully fails to do so, or who knowingly or willfully prevents another person from doing so, shall be guilty of a misdemeanor of the first degree, punishable as provided in s. 775.082, s. 775.083 or s. 775.084." [s. 944.35(6)] F.S.

B. "Any person who knowingly or willfully submits inaccurate, incomplete or untruthful information with regards to reports required shall be guilty of a misdemeanor of the first degree, punishable as provided in s. 775.082, s. 775.083 or s. 775.084 F.S. Any person who knowingly or willfully coerces or threatens any other person with the intent to alter either testimony or a written report regarding an incident where force was used, shall be guilty of a felony of the third degree, punishable as provided in s. 775.082, s. 775.083 or s. 775.084." [s. 944.35(7)] F.S.

C. "Any employee of the department who, with malice afore thought, commits a battery to the person of an inmate shall be guilty of a misdemeanor of the first degree, punishable as provided in s. 775.082, s. 775.083 or s. 775.084 F.S. Any employee of the department who inflicts cruel or inhuman treatment by neglect or otherwise, and in so doing causes great bodily harm, permanent disability, or permanent disfigurement to the person of an inmate shall be guilty of a felony of the third degree, punishable as provided in 775.082, s. 775.083 or s. 775.084 F.S. Notwithstanding prosecution, any violation of the provisions of this section, as determined by the Career Service Commission shall constitute sufficient cause under s. 110.227 F.S. for dismissal from employment with the department, and such person shall not again be employed with the department, and such person shall not again be employed in any capacity in connection with the correctional system." [s. 944.35(3)] F.S.

VIII. Intermediate "Less Than Lethal" Force Alternatives

  A. Chemical agents, electronic restraining devices, and batons are considered to be intermediate Use-of-Force alternatives. Batons shall only be used during situations where a trained Baton Squad has been activated to quell a major disturbance. The decision to use chemical agents or electronic restraining devices shall be based on an assessment as to which level of force is likely to ensure the desired result while also resulting in the least amount of injury to all parties involved. The following guidelines shall be considered when deciding which intermediate level of force to use in those situations when lesser levels of force or persuasion are ineffective:

  1. Hands-on physical force should normally be avoided if less injury is likely to occur by using chemical agents or electronic restraining devices.

  2. Chemical agents shall normally be the initial intermediate level of force alternative to be utilized within the institutions (See Section X "Use of Chemical Agents" for specific guidelines). Depending on the circumstances, however, the use of electronic restraining devices may be more appropriate.

  3. Electronic stun devices shall be the intermediate level of force alternative to be utilized primarily, but not exclusively, during transports and supervision of inmates outside of the institutions (See Section IX "Use of Stun Devices" for specific guidelines).

IX. Use of Electronic Restraining Devices (ERDs)

See Chapter V "Arsenal and Ready Room Equipment" to determine the types of electronic restraining devices that are authorized in the Department.

A. Electronic restraining devices shall not be used except in the following circumstances until all reasonable efforts and lesser levels of force, especially verbalization, have been exhausted:

1. To prevent any unauthorized individual from taking possession of an officer's firearm;

2. To prevent an inmate from physically harming himself or others;

3. To prevent an inmate from escaping;

4. To prevent an inmate from taking a hostage or to help free a hostage;

5. In the case of cell extractions, when it is determined that less injury will result than if other force alternatives are utilized;

6. To gain control of an inmate so that the appropriate restraint devices can be applied.

B. Electronic restraining devices shall only be utilized by officers who have successfully completed the Department of Corrections' authorized training for these devices.

C. Electronic restraining devices shall be utilized in strict accordance with manufacturer's specifications and limitations.

D. Electronic restraining devices shall not:

1. Be used to punish any inmate.

2. Be fired into large metal objects, doing so can cause kick back and a resulting shock.

3. Be used in the presence of combustible materials. An open spark could ignite flammable gases or liquids.

4. Be used if the user's hand, the unit, and/or the inmate are wet. Doing so could cause a shock-back effect.

5. Be used on females who are known to be pregnant.

6. Be applied to the following areas of the body:
   a) Head
   b) Genitals
   c) Female breasts
   d) Onto open wounds or stitches

7. Be used on people with known neuro-muscular diseases:
   a) Multiple Sclerosis
   b) Muscular Dystrophy

8. Be used on people who are less than 80 lbs in weight.

9. Be used against an inmate brandishing a handgun or other firearm or a knife except in extreme emergencies.

10. Be used to threaten or attempt to gain information from an inmate.

11. Be used against an inmate unless physical resistance has to be overcome.

12. Be used to wake up a suspected intoxicated individual.

13. Be used as a prod.

E. The length of each application shall not normally exceed eight (8) seconds.

F. The use of electronic restraining devices within [an] institution shall be authorized only by order of the Superintendent if in the institution, or by his designee if the Superintendent is not available. For purposes of this chapter, the designee shall be of a rank of Shift Supervisor or higher. The Shift Supervisor shall normally be present when electronic restraining devices are used on the compound unless circumstances are such that this is not possible.

1. Where time and circumstances permit, medical staff should be consulted to determine if the inmate has any medical condition that would make the use of an electronic restraining device particularly dangerous.

G. Electronic restraining devices shall be issued to Transport Officers on any trip where firearms are also issued. The Correctional Officer Chief, or in his absence, the Officer-in-Charge shall determine the number of officers who will be issued electronic restraining devices during trips that include close custody inmates. This requirement to have an electronic restraining device as a "back up" (less-than-lethal) alternative to the firearm also applies in outside hospital situations.

H. Electronic restraining devices present an alternative to injurious force and offer four distinct levels of "less-than-lethal" intermediate force. Depending on the circumstances, the lowest level of force required to gain control and to minimize injuries should be utilized in accordance with the following guidelines:

1. Optional compliance (visual test display), normally this alone will act as a deterrent;

2. Repelling (momentary contact);

3. Stunning (duration contact); and

4. Full take down (short term, non-lethal incapacitation).

I. As soon as possible, following each use of an electronic restraining device, the inmate shall be afforded medical examination and treatment.

J. In any case where electronic restraining devices are used, an accurate Use of Force Report shall be written and include:

1. What precipitated the use of the device;

2. To what extent it was used and what results were derived from its use;

3. An indication of the number of and location of marks left by the device; and

4. Color photos of the torso depicting all the application points of the device.

K. Electronic restraining devices (handheld units and shields) shall normally be stored and maintained in either the Main Arsenal or the Control Room Arsenal. The Superintendent may authorize, in writing, the storage of one handheld unit and one shield in the Officer's station in the Confinement Unit. These devices shall be kept secured (locked cabinet) when not in use.

1. The Arsenal Sergeant shall be responsible for the proper maintenance repair and inventory of all electronic restraining devices. Maintenance shall include the testing of devices and changing of batteries in accordance with manufacturer's specifications.

2. All electronic restraining devices shall be signed out/in in the same manner as firearms.

3. There shall be no attempt to alter, tamper with, or repair any electronic restraining device. If a unit appears to need repair or to malfunction, it should be sent to an authorized repair source. If a unit appears to require attention, that unit will not be issued out until repaired and properly functioning. If any electronic restraining device is dropped or knocked out of the hand, upon recovery, it should be immediately tested to determine if it is damaged or is operating properly.

X. Use of Chemical Agents

A. It shall be the policy of the Department that:

1. <u>Chemical agents shall never be used to punish an inmate</u>.

2. No inmate will be removed from his assigned cell and placed into another cell for the purpose of administering chemical agents.

3. No inmate shall be hand cuffed solely for the purpose of administering chemical agents. If chemical agents are administered to a handcuffed inmate, an explanation as to why the removal of the handcuffs was not feasible, shall be included in Section I of the Report of Force Used (DC3-300).

4. No inmate will be stripped of his clothing or comfort items for the explicit purpose of administering chemical agents.

5. Chemical agents shall not be used except when the need to use force is clearly indicated and when this level of force is the least likely to cause injuries to staff or inmates.

6. All chemical agents shall be used with caution and in accordance with the manufacturer's specifications and limitations. The Material Safety Data Sheet (MSDS) shall be maintained and adhered to regarding all the types of chemical agents in use at the institution.

    a) Only those staff properly trained in chemical agent utilization and authorized by the Superintendent or his designee will be allowed to administer chemical agents.

    b) Chemical agents shall not be used at a distance of less than five (5) feet except under circumstances of extreme conditions where this cannot be avoided.

7. In accordance with the procedures outlined in X, C, chemical agents shall be authorized only by order of the Superintendent or a "high ranking" employee specifically designated by the Superintendent. For purposes of this chapter, high ranking means Shift Supervisor or higher.

8. Most chemical agents shall be kept in the Main Arsenal. A small amount of chemical agents may be stored in the Control Room Mini-Arsenal or other secure place until their use or deployment has been authorized.

9. Discharge of chemical agents directly onto an inmate or discharge of large quantities into a confined space, such as a small room, cell, or vehicle, requires examination of any inmate(s) directly exposed by an authorized member of the medical staff, as soon as possible after exposure.

10. In any case where chemical agents are used, an accurate record must be maintained as to what type of agent was used, how much was used, method of administration, persons authorized to draw and administer the agent, location administered and reason for use. This information will be maintained by the employee administering the agent and also be submitted with the Use of Force Report.

B. Explanation/Definitions:

1. See Chapter V "Arsenal and Ready Room Equipment" to determine the types of chemical agent delivery systems that are authorized in the Department.

2. Each type of chemical agent (OC, CN, and CS) is effective in a wide range of circumstances and situations. Each however, has limitations and unique decontamination requirements.

   a) In most indoor situations, authorized OC products should be the first agent to be administered as they are considered to be less harmful and less contaminating than either CN or CS.

   b) Because of the risk of contamination, <u>CS shall be used in buildings only as a last resort</u>.

3. The description of chemical agent types includes:

a) OC (Oleoresin Capsicum)—is classified as an Inflammatory agent, which when employed will immediately cause a swelling of the nasal passages and throat and a burning sensation to the eyes. OC is reportedly more effective than CN or CS when employed against persons who are "high" on drugs and/or alcohol, psychotics, or who are otherwise pain insensitive. OC will not normally vaporize as well as CN or CS and therefore may not permeate all areas of an enclosed or open space as well. This agent is relatively easy to decontaminate.

b) CN (Chloroacetophenone)—is classified as a Lachrymator agent, which when employed takes between 2-5 seconds to cause tearing and profuse nasal discharge. CN reportedly is not as effective as CS nor is it always effective against persons who are "high" on drugs and/ or alcohol, psychotics, or who are otherwise pain insensitive. This agent is relatively easy to decontaminate.

c) CS (Orthochlorbenzalmalononitrile or o-Chlorobenzylidene—Malononitrile) is classified as an Irritant agent, which when employed takes between 20-60 seconds to cause tightening and pain in the chest, vomiting, sneezing, and a closing of the eyes. CS is not always effective against persons who are "high" on drugs and/or alcohol, psychotics, or [those] who are otherwise pain insensitive. This agent is generally difficult to decontaminate.

C. Procedure for the use of Chemical Agents on One or More Inmates That May Be Disruptive:

1. If an inmate becomes disorderly, disruptive, unruly, and all reasonable attempts by officers at counseling and ordering the cessation fails, the Shift Supervisor (or above) shall be contacted for further instructions.

2. If in the assessment of the Shift Supervisor all reasonable efforts to control the disorderly inmate and the administration of chemical agents is the least level of force, that can reasonably be expected to successfully gain control of the disruptive inmates(s), while minimizing the risk of injuries to all involved, he shall:

   a) Where time and circumstances permit, ensure that medical staff are contacted to determine if the inmate has a medical condition that would prevent the use of chemical agents; and

   b) Contact the Superintendent, if in the institution, or his designee, if Superintendent is not available, and request authorization to utilize chemical agents.

3. Prior to using chemical agents, the Superintendent or designee shall ensure that the inmate again is counseled by staff to cease his actions.

   a) If these efforts prove to be futile, the Shift Supervisor shall order the disorderly inmate to cease his actions and inform him that chemical agents will be administered if he continues his disruptive behavior.

   b) Any uninvolved inmates in the cell or immediate area should be given an opportunity to leave the potentially affected area; if so doing will not jeopardize the safety of staff or other inmate.

   c) Except in cases of extreme emergency, the Shift Supervisor should be present during the time of the final counseling period and the administering of chemical agents.

4. Approximately three (3) minutes after the order is given to cease the disorderliness, if the inmate continues his disruptive behavior, chemical agents may be administered in the form of no more than three, one-second bursts. If

physical injury to staff or other inmates appear imminent, spontaneous force in the form of chemical agents may be utilized.

5. If, approximately five (5) minutes after the initial administration of chemical agents, the inmate(s) still continues his disruptive behavior, chemical agents may again be administered in the form of no more than three, one-second bursts.

6. If this second administration of chemical agents fails to control the inmate's disruptive behavior, medical staff should again be consulted to assist in determining the next course of action, which may involve:

   a) Medical/psychological intervention;

   b) An additional administration of the same or of an alternate type of chemical agent (again, no more than three, one-second bursts); or

   c) Use of electronic restraining devices (for use in cell extractions or to gain control of an inmate so that restraints can be safely applied).

7. The inmate(s) shall be examined by medical staff as soon as possible after the chemical agent has been used but not more than one (1) hour after the first exposure, except in cases of great emergency where this may not be possible.

D. In the event of a major disturbance, a chemical agent squad as outlined in Emergency Plans (riot, disorder) may be activated.

E. Decontamination of Personnel and Inmates After Use of Chemical Agents:

   1. Any part of the body exposed to chemical agents, especially eyes, shall be flushed with generous amounts of water as soon as possible after exposure. "Flood" the affected area

of the body for five (5) to ten (10) minutes or until relief is experienced by the affected person.

2. <u>Do not</u> rub the affected area with a cloth or towel or apply oils, creams, or hydrocortisone unless medical so directs.

F. Decontamination of Clothing After use of Chemical Agents:

1. Contaminated clothing shall be laundered separately from uncontaminated clothing. Laundering shall occur using cold water and no soap, using the longest cycle and highest water setting possible.

2. Clothing should be removed before the spin cycle and be allowed to air dry.

3. In the case of CS contamination, if the above procedure does not decontaminate clothing after the first washing and air drying, this clothing should be destroyed by burning.

G. Decontamination of Indoor Areas After use of Chemical Agents:

1. Blankets and sheets should be removed from area and be decontaminated as in X, E.

2. If normal ventilation fails to decontaminate an indoor area, forced ventilation using a fan to push air out of building should be used.

3. In the case of CS contamination, if forced ventilation fails to decontaminate an indoor area, the following solution should be used to scrub the contaminated area:

— Six and two-third pints of Monoethanolamine and fifty-five pints of distilled water and 3 ounces of Tide or Joy.

XI. Use of Firearms

In order for all concerned to be aware of their responsibilities, the following statewide procedures should be included in

Institutional Operating Procedures, Post Orders and Escape
Emergency Plans.

A. No employee shall, in conjunction with his job responsibilities,
    carry a firearm or weapon on or about his person, either
    concealed or unconcealed, unless it is state equipment which
    has been properly issued and employee is acting within the
    scope of official duties with the Department of Corrections.

B. Firearms or weapons will be issued to an employee only
    upon instructions of the Superintendent, Assistant
    Superintendent, Correctional Officer Chief, or the Officer-
    in-Charge through the Arsenal Officer or other officer
    designated to issue weapons.

C. Guidelines for Use of Firearms

    1. Maximum force should never be used on the mere suspicion
       that a crime, no matter how serious, was committed or
       that the person being pursued committed the crime.

    2. Employees shall not intentionally discharge a firearm at
       or in the direction of another human being except under
       the following circumstances and after all reasonable
       non-lethal alternatives have been exhausted, and there is
       no danger to innocent bystanders:

       a) Escapes From Outside a Secure Perimeter:

          (1) When the identified escaped inmate has refused a
              verbal order to stop after being ordered to do so by
              a correctional employee, thus necessitating the
              discharge and firing of a warning shot (circumstances
              permitting). If a warning shot fails or circumstances
              do not permit one, the correctional employee is
              entrusted to shoot to stop the inmate. Although the
              correctional officer is empowered to shoot a fleeing
              escapee, the previous statement in no way implies
              that he must automatically shoot to kill.

b) Escape Attempts From Inside a Secure Perimeter:

(1) In institutions that have a double fence, where possible and time permitting, a verbal warning to halt should occur prior to the inmate touching the inner fence. Time permitting, a warning shot should then be fired prior to the inmate breaching the inner fence. The firearm should not be aimed at the inmate and used to stop him until he has breached the inner fence and is attempting to breach the outer fence.

(2) In institutions that have a single fence, where possible and time permitting, a verbal warning to halt and a warning shot should occur prior to the inmate reaching the perimeter fence. The firearm should not be aimed at the inmate and used to stop him until he has begun to either cut through or climb over the fence.

c) As a last resort only in cases of:

(1) Escape;

(2) Helicopter assisted escapes/assaults

— See Section X(D) for specific instructions;

(3) Use of vehicle to gain unauthorized entry into or exit from a correctional institution—See Section X(E) for specific instructions;

(4) To prevent injury to a person, including self defense; and

(5) To quell a disturbance.

d) Weapons to be used will be designated by the person in charge.

3. Firearms shall not be discharged

a) In any case where there is reason to believe that the life of an innocent bystander will be endangered by discharge of the firearm.

b) From any moving vehicle unless such action is reasonably believed necessary to protect himself or another from imminent death or great bodily harm.

c) As a warning except during escapes unless exceptional circumstances exist which in the sound discretion and good judgment of the employee would fully justify the firing of a warning shot.

d) Until the employee is sure that an escape is occurring and he is reasonably certain that the person to be fired upon is an escapee.

e) Until the employee is sure of the target and what lies beyond.

f) If an inmate is escaping and the officer is recapturing the inmate in a congested area or on a crowded street.

4. Any correctional employee who willfully or wantonly fires or otherwise discharges his weapon carelessly or at random may be prosecuted in accordance with Florida law.

D. Helicopter Assisted Escapes/Assaults

1. Because of the possibility of helicopters being employed to effect an escape or assault, the following procedures shall be implemented when appropriate:

a) A person observing an aircraft flying close to an institution in such a manner that they feel it is a potential threat to the security of the institution shall immediately notify the main control room of the following:

(1) Identification markings of aircraft such as:

    (a) I.D. Number. The properly registered aircraft number will always start with a "N."

    (b) Type of aircraft; fixed wing or helicopter.

    (c) Approximate size of aircraft

    (d) Model—Such as Huey and Cessna.

    (e) Make—Such as Bell and Boeing.

    (f) Color of aircraft—Such as white and red.

    (g) Trim—Such as red over white.

(2) Specific location of aircraft in relation to the institution site, such as southeast corner of recreation yard.

(3) Activities of aircraft, such as attempting to land, hovering, or circling the compound.

(4) Number of persons on board.

(5) Number of inmates in close proximity of aircraft that could possibly board the craft.

(6) Direction of flight, such as from south to north.

b) The main control room shall immediately notify the Senior Correctional Officer on duty, and then the Superintendent's Office. The Senior Correctional Officer on duty will evaluate the situation and place the institution in the appropriate level of alert. If in the opinion of the Senior Correctional Officer on duty the aircraft is a threat to the security of the institution, appropriate armed security staff will be dispatched to the area where the aircraft is located. After notifying the Officer-in-Charge and Superintendent, the Control Room shall contact law enforcement for vehicle "chase" plane assistance, as well as the Federal Aviation Administration giving identifying information as in D,1, a). If it is apparent that the aircraft is attempting to land, the following actions shall occur:

(1) Attempts, other than firing of weapons such as waving of arms in such a manner as to indicate disapproval to enter area, should be made in an attempt to cause the aircraft to leave.

(2) If these attempts fail, allow the aircraft to land.

(3) Keep all inmates away from the aircraft.

(4) Secure the aircraft using armed security staff, if possible.

(5) If the landing was brought about due to an emergency, i.e. engine failure or other, retain security of the aircraft and all occupants until their removal from the site.

(6) If the intrusion is an assault attempt and weapons are fired from the aircraft, Department personnel are authorized to return fire when in the opinion of the officer using force a life threatening situation exists and the use of deadly force is necessary to protect the life and well-being of inmates, staff and other individuals who may be on the compound.

(7) Once the aircraft lands, all efforts should be directed to stop any inmate from boarding the aircraft in an attempt to effect an escape. Staff are authorized to shoot any inmate attempting to effect such an escape in accordance with existing policy with regard to the use of weapons to prevent escapes. When circumstances permit, a verbal warning to halt and a warning shot shall be fired prior to the inmate reaching the aircraft and prior

to shooting at the inmate. Once an inmate is in the aircraft efforts to shoot him shall cease. Staff are not authorized to shoot at an aircraft as it departs the institution unless weapons are being fired from the aircraft or the aircraft continues to present a security risk such as to create a reasonable belief in the officer that a failure to use deadly force would pose a life threatening danger to other inmates, staff, and other individuals who may be on the compound.

(8) Should attempts to prevent inmates from boarding the aircraft described in (7) above fail and the aircraft leaves, immediate notification of the law enforcement agency as well as the Federal Aviation Administration giving present flight direction and reverification of identifying information as in D, 1, a). Additional information on the inmates, damage to the aircraft, and weapons used by criminals should be provided.

(9) All inmates will receive orientation in regard to this policy of the Department. This orientation will contain instructions indicating that should any helicopter or aircraft either attempt to land on or near the property of any Department of Corrections' facility, inmates are required to move away from the aircraft. Movement toward the aircraft by an inmate will be viewed as an escape attempt and will subject the inmate to above indicated conditions.

(10) This policy shall be made a part of the Department's orientation program at all Reception Centers.

2. Incidents involving an aircraft shall immediately be reported by phone to the Federal Aviation Administration

District Office in Orlando, Florida; Phone (407) 648-6840. A follow-up letter providing details of the incident should be provided to:

Federal Aviation Administration
9677 Tradeport Drive
Suite 100
Orlando, Florida 32827

a) Information provided the Federal Aviation Administration should contain all known identification markings of aircraft as well as the date and time of the incident. They have assured us that they will pursue efforts to assist in locating the pilots for possible prosecution.

E. Use of Vehicle(s) to Gain Unauthorized Entry into or Exit from a Correctional Institution:

1. The Department shall take steps to prevent vehicles from being used to gain unauthorized/forced entry into or forced exit from any of its correctional facilities.

2. If it becomes necessary, the following procedure should be followed:

a) Time permitting, a verbal order to halt shall be issued followed by a warning shot if the vehicle fails to stop.

b) If the vehicle continues and it is evident that it is going to ram the perimeter area and will thereby endanger lives of staff and/or inmate; and if there is a clear line of fire, firearms should be used to disable the vehicle.

c) When possible, and time permitting, anytime a shot is fired at a vehicle, it should be aimed at a tire(s) and/or engine with the intent of disabling the vehicle.

F. In all cases, the employee discharging a weapon will file a complete written report of the incident. If any correctional employee has discharged a weapon while responding to an emergency situation, escape, disturbance, or otherwise, the empty cartridges are to be secured, tagged, dated, and signed for the purpose of maintaining accurate information and evidence during future investigation of this incident.

XII. Medical Attention Following Use of Force.

A. In all cases where physical force is used to manage an inmate, the inmate and any employees who are involved should be provided with an opportunity for medical examination. Appropriate medical treatment will be provided immediately if an inmate or employee is injured. Any such treatment or follow-up action shall be documented on Form DC3-300, Report of Force Used.

B. A qualified health care provider shall examine any person physically involved in a use of force to determine the extent of injury, if any, and shall prepare a report in accordance with Health Care procedures. A copy of the report, along with the referenced forms, shall be attached to the Report of Force Used. Such reports shall be submitted to the Superintendent for appropriate review.

Montana Department of Corrections Policies and Procedures

Policy No.: DOC 3.1.8
Subject: USE OF FORCE AND RESTRAINTS
Chapter 3: FACILITY/PROGRAM OPERATIONS
Section 1: Security and Control
Revision Date:
Effective Date: April 1, 1997

I. POLICY:

It is the policy of the Department of Corrections to provide employees with the appropriate training and guidance on the permissible use of force in its facilities, to ensure that force is only used when necessary, and only to the degree necessary to subdue an individual offender, or restore order to a disruptive group in the facility. Deadly force may be used in adult facilities to prevent an escape, prevent the loss of life or serious bodily injury, to protect state property only when its damage or loss would facilitate escape, loss of life, or serious bodily injury, to control riots or disturbances, to prevent offenders from breaching security areas, or to protect the public. The use of force, security equipment, and restraint equipment is intended only as a control measure and when absolutely necessary. These measures are not intended, and will not be used, as a means of punishment. In juvenile correctional facilities/programs, the use of deadly force will only be authorized to prevent the imminent loss of life.

II. AUTHORITY:

53-1-203, MCA. Powers and Duties of the Department

45-3-106, MCA. Use of Force to Prevent Escape

45-3-102, MCA. Use of Force in Defense of Person

III. DEFINITIONS:

Baton means kubaton, extendable baton, and riot baton which may be made of plastic, aluminum, or a similar substance.

Calculated Use of Force means the consideration of an application of the appropriate amount of force to resolve the situation.

Chemical Agents—CN and CS means:
    CN—Chloracetophenone—a lachrymatory agent
    CS—Orthochlorobenzalonoitrate—an irritant agent

Inflammatory Agent means a substance like Oleoresin Capsicum (OC) which is derived from the cayenne pepper plant and classified as an inflammatory agent that affects the mucous membranes and the upper respiratory system.

Continuum Use of Force means applying a progressive level of force used to gain control of an offender, starting with passive counter measures up to and including deadly force. Use of force will be limited to the minimum amount necessary to control the situation.

Deadly Force means any weapon, implement or body movement which carries substantial risk of death or serious injury being inflicted upon the person against whom the force is being directed, including:

1. the firing of a firearm in the direction of a person, even though no purpose exists to kill or inflict serious bodily harm; and

2. the firing of a firearm at a vehicle in which a person is riding.

Documentation means reports such as Institutional Incident Report, Medical, Infraction and Use of Force Information Reports or pictures and/or videotapes of an incident including all information identifying relevant evidence.

Escort Technique means actions to ensure appropriate moderate control of an offender while moving them. These techniques can also be used in the event further control becomes necessary.

Flex Cuffs means temporary restraints made of flexible material to be used during emergency situations, or at times when other restraints are not available.

Immediate Use of Force means actions which staff may immediately take in response to an emergency situation which constitutes a serious threat to the safety of staff, offenders, others, to property, and facility security or order.

Kinetic Stunning Devices means projectile(s) delivered to inflict blunt force designed to temporarily incapacitate.

Mechanical Restraints means devices such as handcuffs, belly chains, and leg irons.

Mental Health Reasons means actions taken for security reasons but in response to suicidal or other behavior by offenders with apparent mental illness.

Passive Counter Measures means techniques/strategies used by staff to gain compliance/control of an offender without forcible physical contact such as:

1. Communications

2. Video-taping of the offender(s)

3. Show of force.

Active Counter Measures means action taken to effectively escort, overcome, or restrain an offender; including:

1. Physical Force

2. Self-Defense Techniques

3. Restraints

4. Oleoresin Capsicum

5. Chemical Agents/Aerosol Irritant

6. Batons

7. Kinetic Stunning Devices

8. Water Hoses.

Restraints means devices designed for the restriction of movement and control of offenders.

Serious Bodily Injury means injury which creates a substantial risk of death or which causes permanent disfigurement or protracted loss or impairment of the function or process of any bodily member or organ.

Show of Force means movement of appropriate staff and/or equipment/weapons to an incident site for the purpose of convincing an offender(s) that adequate staff and measures are available and will be used to successfully resolve the situation.

Soft Restraints means leather, canvas or similar type material utilized for mental health and/or medical reasons.

IV. PROCEDURES:

The use of force is sometimes necessary in the correctional environment for justifiable self-defense, protection of others, protection of property, and prevention of escapes, but only as a last resort. Equipment necessary to the use-of-force applications will be stored and controlled in accordance with Department policy 3.1.7 on armory operations. Force should be employed only to the degree necessary to control the offender, and to the level that will be effective with a minimum of harm to both staff and the offender.

In order to prevent abuse of offenders, and unnecessary injuries to staff or offenders, each facility will have a well developed body of local procedures that regulate the use of force, describes conditions under which force may be used, and emphasizes a realistic evaluation of the actual need for the application of a particular level of force. The Warden/Superintendent/Program Administrator will establish local procedures that govern the use of force, including training for employees and annual qualification for staff, and will negotiate mutual agreements with local law enforcement on the use of deadly force. Only authorized equipment will be used. Except in extreme emergencies, firearms are not permitted inside any Department facility, and only then upon authorization of the Warden/Superintendent/ Program Administrator.

A.   Levels of Force

Staff are expected to know and be able to apply the proper level of force needed to control an offender's behavior. The levels of force available to a staff member are Passive Counter Measures, Active Counter Measures and Deadly Force. Use of force should be limited to the minimum amount necessary to control a situation. Force should not be used as punishment, personal abuse, harassment or coercion.

1. Passive Counter Measures are techniques/strategies used by staff to gain compliance/control of an offender without forcible physical contact, such as:

a. Communications

b. Video-taping of the offender(s)

c. Show of force.

2. <u>Active Counter Measures</u> are justified to subdue unruly offenders, to separate participants in a fight, in self-defense or in defending staff, offenders or other persons, and to move offenders who fail to comply with lawful orders. Staff are authorized to use necessary active counter measures without prior approval under the following or similar conditions which are determined to be "emergency situations":

   a. Self-defense

   b. Defense of another to prevent any type of bodily injury to staff, offender(s) or visitor(s)

   c. Maintenance of security

   d. Prevention of a crime

   e. Prevention of suicide or self-mutilation

   f. Prevention of escape

   g. Destruction of state property.

3. <u>Deadly Force</u>

   The use of potentially deadly force carries the obligation and responsibility to exercise discipline, caution, restraint and good judgment. Staff must keep in mind that the use of potentially deadly force presents a danger to the subject and to innocent parties. Only trained and qualified staff are authorized to use deadly force, and only as a last resort. Deadly force will only be used for the following reasons and only after all reasonable alternatives have been exhausted:

   a. To prevent death or serious injury of any person when no other means of resolving the situation is evident.

b. To prevent escape, if the escape is actually in progress and cannot be reasonably prevented with a lesser degree of force.

c. To protect State property only when its damage or loss would facilitate escape, loss of life, or serious bodily injury.

d. To control riots or disturbances.

e. To prevent offenders from breaching security areas.

The following four conditions or elements must be part of the decision-making process to determine whether the offender's actions constitute the threat of imminent danger of death or serious bodily injury:

a. Ability or Apparent Ability—Does the offender possess the ability or the apparent ability to kill you or a third party? Disparity in size, age, strength, gender, numbers, and the level of aggressiveness of the involved parties are all important factors when considering the element of ability.

b. Opportunity—The officer must reasonably believe that the offender(s) are in a position to bring the destructive powers of their "ability" to bear upon you or a third party. Does the staff believe that s/he (or other person) is within the effective range of the suspect's weapons?

c. Imminent Jeopardy—The offender must be acting in such a manner that a reasonable person would conclude that s/he will likely exercise the power to kill or cause serious bodily injury at any moment.

d. Exhaust all Reasonable Options—The staff member should employ deadly force as a last resort. The conditions must be such, that under the circumstances, the staff member has no reasonable alternative.

Verbal warnings will be used prior to the use of firearms. Unless the situation is immediately life-threatening, a warning shot will be fired before any other shots, but firing of a warning shot is not mandatory. If aimed fire at an offender is necessary, the intention will be to stop. Staff members who are fired upon by an offender or nonoffender may return fire, taking into account the safety of noncombatants who may be in the vicinity. Staff using deadly force will employ all possible caution when in the proximity of civilians or when a fired shot may carry into an inhabited area. Only staff who are weapons-qualified may be issued, or authorized to use firearms in the course of their duties. The Training Unit will ensure applicable state regulations are applied in all training on all approved weapons. Local procedures will describe in detail the location of armed posts, limit weapons from being in contact with offenders, requirements for reporting when weapons have been discharged, as well as necessary training for all types of authorized weapons. Each facility will be required to maintain an up-to-date listing of all staff qualified to use weapons. The Warden/Superintendent/Program Administrator will specify the location, and make regulations regarding the operation of armed posts, including clear restrictions on taking firearms into the secure portion of the facility.

B. The Continuum of Force

Offenders' actions will dictate what level of force staff are authorized to use to control the situation [see attachment A, page 180].

1. Offender Uncooperative—staff respond with Passive Counter Measures: communication, video camera, show of force.

2. Offender Aggressive and may cause physical injury— authorized staff respond with Active Counter Measures: physical force, self-defense techniques, restraints, use of

Oleoresin Capsicum, chemical agents, batons, kinetic stunning devices, water hoses.

3. Offender will probably cause death or serious physical injury to others—authorized staff may respond with Deadly Force: ready weapon, verbal warning to stop, warning shot, shoot to stop.

C. Batons

When the degree of force that can be applied by direct contact alone is inadequate, additional force may be exerted. Batons may be used to separate fighting offenders or to quell other types of violence. Staff will not carry batons during the course of their duties. A supply of batons will be maintained in a secure area designated by the security manager for issue on the authorization of the shift supervisor. Squad tactics may be necessary in responding to incidents in cells or other areas. Staff involved in these activities will be trained in these tactics, as well as the use of batons, shields, and other protective equipment.

D. Restraints

The use of restraint equipment is intended to prevent threats to security, escape, assault, suicide, for mental health reasons, or the commission of some other offense by violent or disruptive offenders, to protect staff and offenders, and under other necessary circumstances approved by the Warden/Superintendent/ Program Administrator or designee.

Adult offenders in maximum security units, or those being placed in temporary lockup (T.L.) status, will be restrained when moved out of their cells for any purpose. Staff in those units may be authorized [sic] handcuffs, with the appropriate controls on the handling of the cuff keys. For offenders in general population units, the use of restraints to control behavior is authorized only when all other reasonable methods have failed. Use of restraints for offenders under escort outside of a correctional facility is discussed in Department policy 3.1.12 on escorted trips.

An offender may be restrained to a medical, or a specially designed bed with the approval of the Warden/Superintendent/ Program Administrator/Medical Doctor. There must be an indication that the offenders' conduct is so violent and dangerous to themselves, or others, that if they remain unrestrained, that they would pose a serious risk to the security and order of the institution. This type of restraint will be done in an area designed to facilitate the safety of staff and the offender. In such cases, specific procedures will ensure that the restraints will be checked every 15 minutes by a medical staff member. An offender so restrained will be given the opportunity to be released from the restraints in order to eat, use the toilet and take care of necessary personal hygiene, or as deemed necessary when their behavior no longer poses a risk to themselves or others.

Restraints should not be applied for longer than eight (8) hours, unless specific suicide or violent behavior is evident. Within twenty-four (24) hours of initiating restraints, the offender should be evaluated in person by a physician, physician assistant, nurse practitioner or psychologist. All incidents requiring the use of restraints to this extent will be immediately reported to the Warden/Superintendent/ Programs Administrator.

The Chief of Security will develop local procedures regarding the use of restraints, and other nonlethal means of restraint, that include use of handcuffs, leg irons, belly chains, black box security devices for handcuffs, and soft restraints. *Electronic Stunning devices are not authorized in Department facilities/program.* Training will be provided in the proper use, and necessary techniques, for each of the devices employed by the respective facility.

E.   Chemical Agents/Inflammatory Agents

The Warden/Superintendent/Programs Administrator or designee may authorize the use of Inflammatory Agents/ Chemical agents to control an offender or group of offenders who otherwise cannot be controlled. The provisions of Department policy 3.1.9 on the use of chemical agents will apply in such circumstances.

F.   Water Hoses

The use of water hoses may be authorized when lesser degrees of force have failed to bring an incident under control. *The decision to employ water hoses will be made only with the approval of the Warden/Superintendent/Program Manager or designee.*

G.   Kinetic Stunning Devices

Less-than-lethal ammunition, such as rubber or wooden projectiles or beanbags are an additional option for controlling violent situations, when approved by the Warden/ Superintendent/Program Manager. While this ammunition does not expose the offenders involved to as great a risk of death or serious injury, it will not be used at close range or directed at the head. Only staff who have received proper training in the use of less-than-lethal ammunition will be authorized to use this equipment.

H.   Follow-Up

In order to ensure that offenders subject to use-of-force techniques are not unduly injured, or to provide necessary treatment after inadvertent injuries, the following procedures will be put into effect:

1.   After active counter measures, or deadly force, has been used against an offender, and particularly when chemical/ inflammatory agents are used, the offender will be

examined by medical staff and receive any necessary intermediate treatment as soon as possible, including the opportunity to shower.

2. If injuries were suffered, further medical attention will be immediately provided.

3. An offender will not be kept in restraints any longer than necessary to control the specific behavior involved.

4. Staff injuries will be treated by institution staff, and a full report will be filed with the Warden/Superintendent/ Program Administrator on the nature and extent of those injuries.

5. Staff will have the option of seeing their personal medical provider either before or after treatment is provided in the facility.

I. Reporting Requirements

The Warden/Superintendent/Program Administrator or designee will be immediately notified when active counter measures, or deadly force, is used, including an accidental weapon discharge. A written report by all staff members involved will be completed no later than the conclusion of that shift, and filed with the Warden/Superintendent/ Program Administrator or designee (see attachment B). A copy will be mailed or faxed to the Legal Unit in Helena. The report will include the following:

- an account of the events leading to the use of force

- an accurate and precise description of the incident and reasons for employing force

- a description of the weapons or devices used, if any, and the manner in which they were employed

- a description of the injuries suffered, if any, and the treatment given or received

- reports of all injuries are to be filed in the offender's central file and the employee's personnel record

- a list of all participants and witnesses to the incident

- a copy of all incident reports compiled as a result of the incident

- a video tape, if applicable, which has been reviewed by the Shift Supervisor

- the Shift Supervisor will prepare a "Use of Force Information Sheet" and attach all incident, medical, and infraction reports, as well as pictures or video tape (see attachment C). These materials and reports shall be reviewed by the Warden/Superintendent or designee on the next working day.

J. Allegations Against Staff

The Warden/Superintendent/Program Administrator, or designee, will investigate all allegations of improper use of force, and will notify the Department of the allegations. In cases where possible criminal acts are involved, the appropriate law enforcement agency will be notified. Department safeguards against unwarranted accusations of this type include videotaping all use of force incidents when possible, and providing safeguards for employee rights in the face of such allegations, including assurances that Miranda rights have been read to the individual in the event that there is a possibility that criminal charges may be filed.

V. CLOSING:

Questions concerning this policy shall be directed to the immediate supervisor.

Attachment A: Continuum of Force

OFFENDER ACTION	FORCE APPLIED	LEVEL OF CONTINUUM
Offender Uncooperative/ will not comply with orders	Communication Video camera Show of force	Passive Counter Measure
Offender Aggressive/ may cause physical injury	Physical force Self-defense techniques Restraints Oleoresin capsicum Chemical agents Batons Kinetic stunning devices Water hoses	Active Counter Measures
1. Serious bodily injury to others 2. Causing death to another 3. Escape 4. Destruction of state property where it could cause loss of life, or escape and serious bodily injury 5. Rioting 6. Breaching security area 7. Imminent loss of life in juvenile facilities	Ready weapon Verbal warning to stop Warning shot* Shoot to stop *Only those staff qualified and authorized to use firearms shall use firearms against offenders	Deadly Force

Attachment B

Department of Corrections Use of Force Information Sheet				
Reporting Shift Commander	Date of Incident		Time of Incident	
Administrator	Notified ( ) Yes ( ) No	Date Notified _____ ( ) N/A	Time Notified _____ ( ) N/A	
On-Scene Supervisor	Incident Videotaped		Incident Photographed	
Video Operator	Photographer		Processed as Evidence	
On-Scene Medical Staff	Time Notified		On-Scene Medical Staff	
Offender	JO/AO Number	Unit	Custody	Race
Type of Force Used: ( ) Immediate ( ) Calculated	Level of Force Applied: ( ) Passive Counter Measure ( ) Active Counter Measure ( ) Deadly		Race Code: I = American Indian A = Asian B = Black W = White H = Hispanic	
STAFF VICTIM _____ _____ _____		OFFENDER VICTIM _____ _____ _____		
UNIT STAFF _____ _____ _____		ADDITIONAL STAFF INVOLVED _____ _____ _____		

Appendix B: Sample Standards on Use of Force—Montana

Attachment C

<table>
<tr><td colspan="5" align="center">

Department of Corrections
Use of Force
Evaluation Report
</td></tr>
<tr><td colspan="3" align="center">Administrator</td><td align="center">Date Reviewed</td><td align="center">Time Reviewed</td></tr>
<tr><td align="center">Offender</td><td align="center">JO/AO Number</td><td align="center">Custody   Race</td><td colspan="2" align="center">Housing Unit</td></tr>
</table>

Race Codes: I = American Indian; A = Asian; B = Black; W = White; H = Hispanic

Level of force properly identified? ( ) Yes ( ) No

If "No," comment: _____

_____

_____

Level of force needed? ( ) Yes ( ) No

If "No," comment: _____

_____

_____

Proper application of force? ( ) Yes ( ) No

If "No," comment: _____

_____

_____

Documentation Reviewed

( ) Video tape   ( ) Shift supervisor's report

( ) Photographs   ( ) Medical evaluation report

( ) On-scene supervisor's report   ( ) Staff Incident report

This Evaluation Committee has Determined

( ) The action taken with respect to the use of force and/or application of force were necessary and reasonable in this situation.

( ) This situation needs further investigation and has been referred to the Department Investigator

Montana Department of Corrections
Policies and Procedures

Policy No.: DOC 3.1.9
Subject: USE OF CHEMICAL AGENTS
Chapter 3: FACILITY/PROGRAM OPERATIONS
Section 1: Security and Control
Revision Date: Oct. 23, 1996
Effective Date: March 1, 1997

I. POLICY:

It is the policy of the Department of Corrections to use the least amount of force available to resolve situations involving confrontation or aggression by offenders. When those means are not effective, chemical agents may be employed to enable staff to subdue an individual offender or to restore order among a disruptive group of offenders.

II. AUTHORITY:

53-1-203, MCA. Powers and Duties of the Department

III. DEFINITIONS:

None

IV. PROCEDURES:

Chemical agents may be used to prevent serious injury or loss of life, prevent or suppress riots or disturbances that may escalate in intensity, or to prevent extensive, willful destruction of state property. These agents will be stored and controlled in accordance with the provisions of Department policies 3.1.7 and 3.1.8 on armory operations and the use of force. If order cannot be restored by application of less forceful methods, chemical agents may be deployed against either individuals or groups of offenders in the form of aerosol, canister, projectile, or engine-powered dispensers.

A. Authorization for Use

The Warden/Superintendent/Program Administrator or designee will typically be the person authorizing the use of any chemical agents in the facility. In an emergency during which these individuals cannot be contacted quickly enough to obtain concurrence, the shift supervisor may authorize the use of chemical agents. The shift supervisor will be present at the scene, and will make a final assessment of the situation before authorizing deployment of the chemical agent. Except in extreme emergencies, offenders will always be given verbal orders to comply or surrender before chemical agents are deployed. When possible, forced air ventilation systems will be shut off to reduce the dispersal of chemical agents to other unaffected portions of the facility.

B. Types of Agents

The following categories of chemical agents may be used:

- <u>CN Gas</u>: This compound will typically be used for indoor applications.

- <u>CS Gas</u>: This compound is highly irritating, and in closed environments has the potential to cause serious medical damage to offenders; its use is generally restricted to outdoor applications.

- <u>Oleoresin Capsicum (OC)</u>: These hand-held chemical agent dispensers may be used in short, controlled bursts in indoor or outdoor applications.

- <u>Smoke compounds</u>: These compounds are ordinarily employed as a supplement to tactical maneuvers and as such they will usually be part of an overall riot control plan, rather than isolated action to restraint [sic] or subdue a single offender.

C. Administrative Safeguards

The following safeguards are necessary to ensure against abuse of chemical agents, particularly OC dispensers:

*   Hand-held dispensers may be kept in locked housing units when authorized by the Warden/Superintendent/ Program Administrator or designee.

*   Individual staff members will not be permitted to carry or use in the facility any commercially available irritant or compound similar to those used by the facility for that purpose.

*   The issue of chemical agents from the armory will be restricted to staff authorized to access this area, and issued only by the armorer or shift supervisor.

*   Chemical agents kept in the control center for emergency use will only be issued on the order of the shift supervisor, except when in the judgment of the unit supervisor the immediate issue and use is necessary, and the shift supervisor is not available. In the event that action of this type is warranted, the unit supervisor must file a report with the Warden/Superintendent/Program Administrator.

*   Staff will videotape all incidents involving the use of chemical agents when possible.

D. Reporting Requirements

A complete report will be filed with the Warden/Superintendent/ Program Administrator when chemical agents are used under any circumstances in the facility. The report, compiled by the shift supervisor, will include, at a minimum, the following:

- written accounts from staff involved in the initial episode, and any witnesses, to be filed prior to the end of the work shift during which the incident took place

- a report by the shift supervisor of the situation and the action taken prior to the use of chemical agents

- copies of reports filed by the medical staff as a follow-up to the incident regarding treatment of staff and offenders

- copies of any incident reports filed against the offender(s) involved

- a notation regarding any referral to local law enforcement authorities for prosecution

- copies of any tapes or photos of the incident or injuries sustained.

E. Follow-up

Offenders who have been subjected to chemical agents may suffer skin, eye, or lung damage and should be removed from the gaseous environment as soon as possible. Offenders who have been subjected to chemical agents will be allowed to change clothes and shower once they are fully under staff control, and, in the judgment of the supervisor, there is no remaining risk to staff. All individuals exposed to chemical agents will be examined by a health care employee as soon as practical. If there are any persistent symptoms of the chemical agent, the offender's condition will be monitored until no further effects or symptoms remain. Cells and other areas exposed to chemical agents may require hosing or other decontamination.

V. CLOSING:

Questions concerning this policy shall be directed to the immediate supervisor.

Montana Department of Corrections
Policies and Procedures

Policy No.: DOC 3.1.10
Subject: USE OF OLEORESIN CAPSICUM SPRAY IN COMMUNITY CORRECTIONS FACILITIES/PROGRAMS
Chapter 3: FACILITY/PROGRAM OPERATIONS
Section 1: Security and Control
Revision Date:
Effective Date: April 1, 1997

I. POLICY:

It is the policy of the Department of Corrections to use the least amount of force necessary to resolve confrontation or aggression by offenders. The use of Oleoresin Capsicum (OC) Aerosol Spray will be governed by this policy.

II. AUTHORITY:

53-3-203, MCA. Powers and Duties of the Department.

III. DEFINITIONS:

Oleoresin Capsicum (OC) means a derivative of Cayenne pepper which is classified as an inflammatory agent. OC exposure generally has the following characteristics:

• works quickly

• symptomatic results may last up to 45 minutes

• there are no documented long lasting harmful effects to the person who is sprayed with OC.

Non-Flammable Propellant means a propellant or delivery system that will not enhance an open flame or cause a fire from a spark.

IV. PROCEDURES:

Trained staff may be issued OC Spray to defend themselves from combative, resisting, and/or violent individuals while reducing the risk of inflicting or receiving injury. OC is not necessarily a replacement or substitute for other authorized devices and techniques and therefore should only be used when it is the best choice for the circumstances. OC is another alternative that can be used at the discretion of staff when the decision is made that the use of force is reasonable under the circumstances.

A. Approval of OC Products

OC products will be approved by the Regional Administrator or Program Administrator of a Community Corrections program/facility.

B. Training

Staff who use OC must successfully complete a Department approved training program prior to being issued OC and recertification will be conducted every two years thereafter. The training will include, but is not limited to:

1. Tactical use and applications of OC

2. Effects of OC use

3. Use of force continuum and policy

4. Decontamination procedures.

C. Use

1. OC may be carried by trained and certified staff as authorized by the program or Regional Administrator.

2. OC may be used in the following situations:

a. Where verbal direction is ineffective or inappropriate.

b. Where passive resistance techniques have failed and staff may have to use physical force to maintain control.

    c. Where the staff could reasonably use deadly force.

    d. Where the offender has refused to come out of a locked building, room, or vehicle.

    e. Where the staff is threatened by domestic or wild animals.

    f. Other situations where training and experience may dictate the use of OC.

3. The use of OC shall be consistent with any applicable state or federal law, the guidelines for the Department's Use of Force policies, and the manufacturer's specific guidelines for usage.

D.   Guidelines for OC Use

1. Staff should only use the amount of OC reasonably needed to achieve the desired effects. Once the desired effect is achieved, use of additional OC must be discontinued.

2. Primary OC application targets include the face, eyes, nose, and mouth.

3. Staff may spray a restrained and combative offender only when other available means of control have been exhausted or would be ineffective.

4. When staff is confronted by an individual who is wielding, or threatening to use an OC aerosol, it must be understood that if the person is successful in spraying the staff member, he/she may be incapacitated for up to 45 minutes. It is foreseeable, and reasonable, to believe that during this time the staff member may be disarmed, killed, or seriously injured by the person, their companions or others. Use, or threat of use, of OC spray upon staff may constitute use of additional force necessary to prevent incapacitation of the staff member.

E. Oleoresin Capsicum Decontamination Procedures

1. After control has been established and/or resistance has ceased, staff will make reasonable efforts to allow the OC-affected subject relief from the discomfort associated with the application of OC.

2. Reasonable OC decontamination efforts may include (as practical under the circumstances of the exposure):

a. Providing fresh air or some other form of ventilation.

b. Flushing the exposed area with clear water.

c. Removing the majority of the OC with a paper towel or cloth.

3. If decontamination cannot be reasonably accomplished in the field, it should be accomplished as soon as practical at the location to which the person is being transported or held.

4. Staff should arrange for immediate medical response if the affected person has extended difficulty breathing or exhibits any other symptoms that staff reasonably believes would require medical attention.

F. Documentation

A complete report shall be filed within 24 hours with the Regional or Program/Facility Administrator or immediate supervisor when OC is used. The report shall include, at a minimum:

1. date and time of OC use

2. a list of all participants and witnesses to the incident

3. an accounting of the events leading to the use of OC

4. a description of the incident and reasons for using OC

5. a description of any injuries suffered and the treatment given/received.

G. Storage and Security of OC Canisters

All staff issued OC canisters will ensure the security of the canisters when carrying them and will store them in secure locations otherwise.

H. Maintenance

Designated facility/program staff will be assigned the responsibility for inspecting the OC units on an annual basis for erosion, leakage, nozzle blockage and fullness. Any damaged units should be replaced immediately.

V. CLOSING:

Questions concerning this policy shall be directed to the Administrator of the Community Corrections Division.

Montana Department of Corrections Policies and Procedures

Policy No.: DOC 3.1.12
Subject: ESCORTED TRIPS
Chapter 3: FACILITY/PROGRAM OPERATIONS
Section 1: Security and Control
Revision Date:
Effective Date: April 1, 1997

I. POLICY:

It is the policy of the Department of Corrections to provide the necessary level of security, supervision and control for offenders who must be escorted outside the facility and in the community.

II. AUTHORITY:

53-1-203, MCA. Powers and Duties of the Department

III. DEFINITIONS:

Chief of Security means the person designated by the Superintendent/ Warden/Program Manager as responsible for the management of the facility's security program and operations.

IV. PROCEDURES:

Offenders being escorted outside of correctional facilities/programs will be transported in a safe and humane manner under the supervision of trained employees. The primary responsibility of staff escorting offenders is public safety. Due to the differences that exist in different correctional facilities/programs, the practices that are outlined in this policy will be tailored to meet the individual facility/program needs.

[Note: the only sections of this policy that relate to use of force include the following—the other parts of this policy have been deleted]

A. Referral and Review

The Chief of Security or designee will:

1. Review all requests for escorting an offender into the community for medical treatment or for other purposes authorized by the facility/program Administrator.

2. Confer with the referring employee, except for regularly scheduled transfer activities, to ascertain the exact nature of the treatment or activity, the expected duration, and the degree of public contact likely in the community setting.

3. Review the relevant materials with a bearing on the type of escort to be provided.

4. Annotate the record to indicate the purpose, time and place of the trip, and identify the staff providing the escort.

5. Have staff develop and document any information necessary to assure a complete review of any special cases.

6. Discuss with the respective Division Administrator or Director the movement of a high profile offender whose case presents the potential for attracting publicity or other attention should the offender be in the community.

7. Authorize the use of a solo staff member to escort an offender who is not an escape or management risk; otherwise, two staff members will escort the offender. Local policy will address the carrying of firearms on escorted trips.

B. Escort Instructions

Staff members selected for escort duty will be advised in writing of the responsibilities of their assignment. That advisement will consist of a locally developed form that contains, at a minimum, the following:

- the name of the offender,

- basic sentence data,

- the itinerary and expected duration of the trip,

- any special escort or supervision instructions,

- the name of the authorizing official, and

- a photograph (optional).

Escort officers will be provided the opportunity to review the offender's file. Staff who will be carrying weapons must be authorized and be weapons qualified. The Chief of Security or designee will provide any additional verbal instructions regarding the trip prior to departure.

C. Searches

1. Exiting the Facility:

Each facility/program will develop specific criteria for the exit procedures of offenders in transport status. These procedures should include the process for searching and restraining offenders per custody classification.

The following outlines the minimum procedures necessary for searching offenders departing the facility under escort: *[Sections a, b, c, e deleted]*

d. The staff escorting the offenders will pat search them before placing them in restraints.

f. The use of restraints for an offender who is not an escape or a management risk will be at the discretion of the Chief of Security or designee.

2. Entering the Facility:

Each facility/program will establish procedures to be followed when an offender is returned from an escorted transport.

D. Restraints

1. The use of restraints, i.e., handcuffs, leg irons, or restraining chains, must be done humanely and only when necessary.

2. Restraining equipment must never be used as punishment, in a way that causes undue physical pain, or to restrict the blood circulation or breathing of an offender.

3. Offenders under escort ordinarily will be in hard restraints, consisting of handcuffs and a waist chain. The decision regarding handcuffing and restraining offenders under escort is delegated to the Chief of Security. Factors to be considered include the following:

a. security classification of the offender (a minimum security offender being transported alone may be in lesser or no restraints)

b. anticipated contact with the public

    c. physical and mental health of the offender

    d. demonstrated behavior of the offender

    e. purpose and destination of trip

    f. mode of travel.

4. The Facility/Program Administrator may authorize additional restraints for cases that present potentially greater escape or management risks.

5. Under no circumstances shall the offender be secured to the vehicle.

E.   Mental Health Transports and Restraints

Mental health cases recommended by medical staff for soft restraints will be carefully reviewed by the Chief of Security before authorizing transport. In those cases, the escorting staff will take hard restraints with them in the event the offender begins to destroy or otherwise compromise the soft restraints. Medical approval will be obtained if it appears that restraint equipment, such as soft or hard restraints, will be necessary to prevent self-mutilation during transfer to a mental health facility. If the offender must be so restrained on an emergency basis, the Medical Supervisor will be notified at the earliest opportunity. Medical staff may be assigned to accompany the offender, and when present will examine the offender at regular and frequent intervals throughout the trip. The escorting officer will confer with the Chief of Security before removing any restraints in the course of medical treatment, unless a life-threatening medical emergency is in progress. In those cases, the escorting staff should explore all possible options before permitting the offender to be completely unrestrained.

F. Weapons Issued During Transportation

When armed supervision is necessary to transport offenders outside the facility, staff that are armed must be securely separated from the offenders (i.e., in secure cubicles in buses, in vehicles preceding or following the offenders' transport, or by a law enforcement-grade barrier in the vehicle). Armed staff should disembark from the vehicles before offenders; staff will then station themselves at a safe distance, but in positions that ensure clear observation of disembarking offenders.

G. Vehicles

Escorted trips typically will be conducted using vehicles equipped with a law enforcement-type barrier between the front and rear seats, and in which the window and door lock mechanisms have been deactivated in the rear of the vehicle. In exceptional cases, a second vehicle with additional staff may accompany the vehicle transporting the offender. Factors to be considered include the following:

1. security classification of the offender (a minimum security offender being transported alone may be in lesser or no restraints and in an uncaged vehicle)

2. anticipated contact with the public

3. physical and mental health of the offender

4. demonstrated behavior of the offender

5. purpose and destination of trip

H. Contact with the Public

While in the community with an offender, the escorting staff will make every attempt to maintain a low profile and avoid public contact. Offenders will not be permitted to make phone calls or otherwise contact family members or others while under escort. Unless specifically authorized by medical staff and facility/program warden/superintendent administrator, hospitalized offenders will not be permitted visitors and/or telephone privileges.

V. CLOSING:

Questions concerning this policy shall be directed to the immediate supervisor.

U.S. Department of Justice
Federal Bureau of Prisons
Program Statement
OPI: CPD
NUMBER: 5566.05
DATE: July 26, 1996
SUBJECT: Use of Force and Application of Restraints on Inmates
[Bracketed Bold—Rules]
Regular Type—Implementing Information

1. [PURPOSE AND SCOPE §552.20. The Bureau of Prisons authorizes staff to use force only as a last alternative after all other reasonable efforts to resolve a situation have failed. When authorized, staff must use only that amount of force necessary to gain control of the inmate, to protect and ensure the safety of inmates, staff and others, to prevent serious property damage and to ensure institution security and good order. Staff are authorized to apply physical restraints necessary to gain control of an inmate who appears to be dangerous because the inmate:

   a. Assaults another individual;

   b. Destroys government property;

   c. Attempts suicide;

   d. Inflicts injury upon self; or

   e. Becomes violent or displays signs of imminent violence.

   This rule on application of restraints does not restrict the use of restraints in situations requiring precautionary restraints, particularly in the movement or transfer of inmates (e.g., the use of handcuffs in moving inmates to and from a cell in

detention, escorting an inmate to a Special Housing Unit pending investigation, etc.)]

Another example of a situation in which precautionary restraints may be used without being subject to the provisions of this Program Statement is when they are applied by medical staff for medical purposes in accordance with procedures set forth in the Health Services Manual.

The use of restraints for psychiatric reasons, (e.g., to prevent suicide or the infliction of self-injury), however, is subject to the provisions of this Program Statement.

This rule's purpose is not to discourage employees from using force when it is necessary, but to provide guidance and instruction on appropriate procedures to follow when confronted with a situation requiring the use of force.

2. PROGRAM OBJECTIVES. The expected results of this program are:

    a. Force will ordinarily be used only when attempts to gain voluntary cooperation have not been successful.

    b. When force is used, it will be only that which is necessary to subdue an inmate or preserve or restore institution security and good order.

    c. Confrontation avoidance techniques will be used when feasible to avoid calculated use of force situations.

    d. When an inmate must be subdued, the use-of-force team technique will be used when feasible.

    e. Any inmate restrained to a bed will be checked every 15 minutes.

    f. Chemical agents will be used as specified and only after a review of the inmate's medical file.

g. Restraints will be applied only for appropriate purposes and in appropriate ways.

h. Appropriate staff will be trained in confrontation avoidance, use of force team technique, use of chemical agents, and application of restraints.

i. Every use of force incident will be appropriately documented, reported, and reviewed.

3. DIRECTIVES AFFECTED

a. Directive Rescinded

PS 5566.04   Use of Force and Application of Restraints on Inmates (06/13/94)

b. Directives Referenced

PS 1380.05   Special Investigative Supervisors Manual (08/01/95)

PS 5214.03   Procedures for Handling of HIV Positive Inmates Who Pose Danger to Others (10/02/87)

PS 5500.07   Correctional Services Manual (01/31/95)

PS 5558.12   Firearms and Badges (06/07/96)

PS 5558.09   Use of Federal 203-A Gas Gun with Zuriel Adapter (Stun Gun) (06/01/92)

PS 6000.04   Health Services Manual (12/15/94)

c. Rules cited in this Program Statement are contained in 28 CFR 552.20-27.

4. STANDARDS REFERENCED

a. American Correctional Association Foundation/Core Standards for Adult Correctional Institutions: FC2-4044, FC2-4046, FC2-4047, FC2-4054, C2-4094.

b.   American Correctional Association 3rd Edition Standards
     for Adult Correctional Institutions: 3-4183, 3-4183-1,
     3-4191, 3-4194, 3-4195, 3-4198.

c.   American Correctional Association Foundation/Core
     Standards for Adult Local Detention Facilities: FC2-5054,
     FC2-5055, C2-5124, C2-5127, C2-5128.

d.   American Correctional Association 3rd Edition Standards
     for Adult Local Detention Facilities: 3-ALDF: 3A-17,
     3A-17-1, 3A-25, 3A-28, 3A-29, 3A-30.

e.   American Correctional Association 2nd Edition Standards for
     the Administration of Correctional Agencies: 2-CO-3A-01.

5. **[TYPES OF FORCE §552.21.]** Since inmates occasionally
    become violent or display signs of imminent violence, it is
    sometimes necessary for staff to use force and restraints to
    prevent them from hurting themselves, staff, or others, and/or
    from destroying property.

    **[a.   Immediate Use of Force. Staff may immediately use force
    and/or apply restraints when the behavior described in
    §552.20 constitutes an immediate, serious threat to the
    inmate, staff, others, property, or to institution security
    and good order.]**

    Section 552.20 refers to Section 1 of this Program Statement.

    In an immediate use of force situation, staff may respond with or
    without the presence or direction of a supervisor.

    **[b.   Calculated Use of Force and/or Application of Restraints.
    This occurs in situations where an inmate is in an area
    that can be isolated (e.g., a locked cell, a range) and
    where there is no immediate, direct threat to the inmate
    or others. When there is time for the calculated use of
    force or application of restraints, staff must first determine
    if the situation can be resolved without resorting to force
    (see §552.23).]**

Section 552.23 refers to Section 7 of this Program Statement.

(1) Circumstances. Based on experience, calculated rather than immediate use of force is feasible in the majority of incidents correctional practitioners encounter. Staff must use common sense and good correctional judgment in each situation to determine when there is time for the calculated use of force.

The safety of persons involved is the major concern. Obviously, immediate (and unplanned) use of force by staff is required if an inmate is trying to self-inflict life-threatening injuries, or is attacking a staff member or another inmate. If those circumstances are not present, staff should ordinarily employ the principles of calculated use of force.

Calculated use of force would be appropriate, for example, if the inmate is in a cell or in an area where the door or grille is (or can be) secured, even where an inmate is verbalizing threats or brandishing a weapon, provided staff believe there is no immediate danger of the inmate hurting self or others. The calculated use of force situation permits the use of other staff (e.g., psychologists, counselors) in attempting to resolve situations in a non-confrontational manner.

(2) Documentation. The confrontation avoidance process will be documented in writing for placement in the inmate's central file, and will be videotaped to include an introduction of all staff participating in the confrontation avoidance group and the actual confrontation avoidance process.

This tape and documentation will be made part of the investigation package for the After Action Review process (see Sections 15 and 16). Additionally, the Warden shall forward each videotape of each incident where force is used to the appropriate Regional Director, within four working days of the incident unless requested earlier by the Regional Director.

The entire interaction shall be documented in writing in the FOI Exempt section of the inmate's central file to reflect each staff member's actions and response while participating in the confrontation avoidance process.

[c. Use of Force Team Technique. If use of force is determined to be necessary, and other means of gaining control of an inmate are deemed inappropriate or ineffective, then the Use of Force Team Technique shall be used to control the inmate and to apply soft restraints, to include ambulatory restraints. The Use of Force Team Technique ordinarily involves trained staff, clothed in protective gear, who enter the inmate's area in tandem, each with a coordinated responsibility for helping achieve immediate control of the inmate.]

See the Correctional Services Manual, Chapter 2, Section 206 (page 11) Use of Force Team Techniques.

[d. Exceptions. Any exception to procedures outlined in this rule is prohibited, except where the facts and circumstances known to the staff member would warrant a person using sound correctional judgment to reasonably believe other action is necessary (as a last resort) to prevent serious physical injury, or serious property damage which would immediately endanger the safety of staff, inmates, or others.]

Use of Force incidents shall be documented and reviewed, and if the provisions of this directive are violated, such review shall also determine if a person using sound correctional judgment would reasonably believe the situation required an exceptional response and if the actions taken were reasonable and appropriate. The Warden (or Acting Warden), Associate Warden (over Correctional Services), Captain, and Health Services Administrator or designee shall comprise the After-Action Review Team reviewing the incident on the next work day after the incident (see Section 16).

The Warden shall personally document to the Regional Director within two work days after the inmate has been released from restraints (if applicable), that the review has occurred and that the use of force was either appropriate or inappropriate. This rule applies to all instances involving the use of force, except for the use of firearms (see the Program Statements on Firearms and Badges and the Correctional Services Manual for more specific procedures on Use of Force Team Techniques).

6. **[PRINCIPLES GOVERNING THE USE OF FORCE AND APPLICATION OF RESTRAINTS §552.22**

   a. **Staff ordinarily shall first attempt to gain the inmate's voluntary cooperation before using force.]**

   See Section 7 of this Program Statement for confrontation avoidance procedures prior to any calculated use of force.

   [b. Force may not be used to punish an inmate.

   c. **Staff shall use only that amount of force necessary to gain control of the inmate. Situations when an appropriate amount of force may be warranted include, but are not limited to:**

   (1) **Defense or protection of self or others;**

   (2) **Enforcement of institutional regulations; and**

   (3) **The prevention of a crime or apprehension of one who has committed a crime.**

   d. **When immediate use of restraints is indicated, staff may temporarily apply such restraints to an inmate to prevent that inmate from hurting self, staff, or others, and/or to prevent serious property damage. When the temporary application of restraints is determined necessary, and after staff have gained control of the inmate, the Warden or designee is to be notified immediately for a decision on whether the use of restraints should continue.]**

Restraints should be used only when other effective means of control have failed or are impractical.

Designee refers to the Acting Warden or Administrative Duty officer.

[e. Staff may apply restraints (for example, handcuffs) to the inmate who continues to resist after staff achieve physical control of the inmate, and may apply restraints to any inmate who is placed under control by the Use of Force Team Technique. If an inmate in a forcible restraint situation refuses to move to another area on his own, staff may physically move that inmate by lifting and carrying the inmate to the appropriate destination.]

Staff are cautioned not to use the restraints for lifting or carrying an inmate.

[f. Restraints should remain on the inmate until self-control is regainegd.

g. Except when the immediate use of restraints is required for control of the inmate, staff may apply restraints to, or continue the use of progressive restraints on, an inmate while in a cell in administrative detention or disciplinary segregation only with approval of the Warden or designee.

h. Restraint equipment or devices (e.g., handcuffs) may not be used in any of the following ways:

   (1) As a method of punishing an inmate;

   (2) About an inmate's neck or face, or in any manner which restricts blood circulation or obstructs the inmate's airways;]

Tape should not be placed around an inmate's mouth, nose, or neck. Staff protective gear provides sufficient insulation from an inmate's spitting or biting; therefore, no effort should be made by use of towels, sheets, blankets, hosiery, or masks or any other device to prevent an innate from spitting or biting.

[(3) In a manner that causes unnecessary physical pain or extreme discomfort;]

Staff in general, and the Lieutenant-in-charge in particular, shall ensure that unnecessary pressure is not placed on an inmate's body in applying restraints (for example, the inmate's chest, back or neck).

While the proper application of restraints may result in some discomfort, examples of prohibited uses of restraints would include, but are not limited to: hog-tying, unnecessarily tight restraints, or improperly applied restraints. All inmates placed in restraints should be closely monitored.

Hard restraints (i.e., steel handcuffs and leg irons) are to be used only after soft restraints prove ineffective, or a past history of ineffectiveness exists.

[(4) To secure an inmate to a fixed object, such as a cell door or cell grill, except as provided in §552.24.]

Section 552.24 refers to Section 10 of this Program Statement.

[i. Medication may not be used as a restraint solely for security purposes.

j. All incidents involving the use of force and the application of restraints (as specified in §552.27) must be carefully documented.]

Section 552.27 refers to Section 15 of this Program Statement. This documentation includes, whenever practicable, filming the incident and having it reviewed by the After-Action Review Committee of the institution. Reports and videotapes of the incident must be reviewed, audited, and monitored by Regional and Central Office staff.

Use of force incidents must be reported and investigated both to protect staff from unfounded allegations and to eliminate the unwarranted use of force.

7. **[CONFRONTATION AVOIDANCE PROCEDURES §552.23. Prior to any calculated use of force, the ranking custodial official (ordinarily the Captain or shift Lieutenant), a designated mental health professional, and others shall confer and gather pertinent information about the inmate and the immediate situation. Based on their assessment of that information, they shall identify a staff member(s) to attempt to obtain the inmate's voluntary cooperation and, using the knowledge they have gained about the inmate and the incident, determine if use of force is necessary.]**

Ordinarily, in calculated use of force situations, there is time for the Captain or Shift Lieutenant, the designated mental health professional, Chaplain, or anyone else so designated, such as the inmate's Unit Manager, Case Manager, or Counselor, to confer with each other and to assess the situation.

This discussion may be accomplished by telephone or in person, the purpose being to gather relevant information about the inmate's medical/mental history, any recent incident reports or situations which may be contributing to the inmate's present state of mind (e.g., a pending criminal prosecution or sentencing, the recent death of a loved one, or a divorce).

This assessment could include discussions with staff who are familiar with the inmate's background or present status. This information may provide insight into the cause of the inmate's immediate agitation, and assist in the identification of staff members who may have some rapport with the inmate, or who are more likely to be successful in attempting to reason with the inmate.

8. USE OF FORCE SAFEGUARDS. To prevent injury and exposure to communicable disease in calculated use of force situations, the following shall occur.

   a. Staff participating in any calculated use of force, including those participating in the Use of Force Team technique, shall:

       (1)   Wear appropriate protective gear, and

       (2)   Receive training on communicable diseases during Annual Refresher Training.

   b.   Personnel with a skin disease or skin injury shall not be permitted to participate in a calculated use of force action.

   c.   Whenever possible, in an immediate use of force circumstance, staff should obtain and use appropriate protective equipment (helmets with face shields, jumpsuits, gloves, pads, etc.) prior to intervening:

       (1)   If an emergency situation results in a use of force, precautions such as clothing help to decrease the chances of transmission.

       (2)   Any time staff members are going into a cell or area where there is reason to believe that blood or body fluids would be present, protective devices shall be available and shall be used by those staff entering that area.

   d.   Following any use of force incident, any area where there is spillage of blood, or other body fluids, shall be sanitized immediately upon the authorization of the Special Investigative Supervisor (SIS) or Shift Supervisor, who must first make the determination as to whether there is a need to preserve evidence.

       (1)   All blood and body secretions shall be immediately removed in an appropriate waste disposal container and the area washed with an antiseptic solution, pursuant to the Program Statement on Procedures for Handling of HIV Positive Inmates Who Pose a Danger to Others and the Health Services Manual.

       (2)   Standard sanitation measures should be implemented following any use of force incident where there has been a spillage of blood or other body fluids by any

inmate or staff member involved. Staff or inmates wearing protective gloves should immediately sanitize the cell walls or floors, etc., with an appropriate disinfectant. In addition, any clothing that has been contaminated with these fluids, including the equipment and clothing of the staff involved in the use of force, should be immediately disinfected or destroyed, as appropriate.

9. PROGRESSIVE AND AMBULATORY RESTRAINTS. For the purposes of this Program Statement, progressive restraints are defined as the process of using the least restrictive restraint method to control the inmate as deemed necessary for the situation. Based on the inmate's behavior, more restrictive and secure restraints may be used. Ambulatory restraints are defined as approved soft and hard restraint equipment which allow the inmate to eat, drink, and take care of basic human needs without staff intervention.

When it is necessary to restrain an inmate for longer than eight hours, the Regional Director or Regional Duty Officer is to be notified telephonically by the Warden or designee or institution Administrative Duty Officer.

Ambulatory restraints should initially be used to restrain an inmate if deemed appropriate for the situation. If the situation dictates the need for more restrictive or secure restraints, based on the inmate's behavior, staff should make the determination as to what form of restraint method should be used; i.e., hard restraints without waist chain or waist belt, hard restraints with waist chain or waist belt, four-point soft restraints with hard restraints used for securing the inmate to the bed, and finally, four-point hard restraints.

In situations involving highly assaultive and aggressive inmates, progressive restraints may be used as an intermediate measure in placing the inmate into, or removing an inmate from, four-point restraints.

10. [USE OF FOUR-POINT RESTRAINTS §552.24. When the Warden determines that four-point restraints are the only means available to obtain and maintain control over an inmate, the following procedures must be followed:

   a. Soft restraints (e.g., vinyl) must be used to restrain an inmate, unless:

      (1) such restraints previously have proven ineffective with respect to that inmate, or

      (2) such restraints are proven ineffective during the initial application procedure.]

This may not be delegated below the Warden's level.

   [b. Inmates will be dressed in clothing appropriate to the temperature.

   c. Beds will be covered with a mattress, and a blanket/ sheet will be provided to the inmate.]

Under no circumstance shall an inmate be allowed to remain naked or without bed covering placed over the inmate's body unless determined necessary by qualified health personnel.

   [d. Staff shall check the inmate at least every 15 minutes, both to ensure that the restraints are not hampering circulation and for the general welfare of the inmate. When an inmate is restrained to a bed, staff shall periodically rotate the inmate's position to avoid soreness or stiffness.]

Qualified health personnel shall evaluate the inmate to be restrained to a bed to determine the position the inmate should be placed in. When qualified health personnel are not immediately available, the inmate shall be placed in a "face-up" position until evaluated by qualified health personnel. Inmates shall be checked every 15 minutes and this information shall be documented.

   [e. A review of the inmate's placement in four-point restraints shall be made by a Lieutenant every two hours to determine if the use of restraints has had the required calming effect and so that the inmate may be released from these restraints (completely or to lesser restraints) as soon as possible. At every two-hour review, the inmate will be afforded the opportunity to use the toilet, unless the inmate is continuing to actively resist or becomes violent while being released from the restraints for this purpose.]

Ordinarily, the Shift Lieutenant makes the decision to release an inmate or apply lesser restraints. It shall never be delegated below the Lieutenant's level.

[f.   When the inmate is placed in four-point restraints, qualified health personnel shall initially assess the inmate to ensure appropriate breathing and response (physical or verbal). Staff shall also ensure that the restraints have not restricted or impaired the inmate's circulation. When inmates are so restrained, qualified health personnel ordinarily are to visit the inmate at least twice during each eight-hour shift. Use of four-point restraints beyond eight hours requires the supervision of qualified health personnel. Mental health and qualified health personnel may be asked for advice regarding the appropriate time for removal of the restraints.]

In institutions without 24-hour medical coverage, the Shift Lieutenant shall ordinarily conduct the checks, if medical coverage is not available. This does not apply to the use of four-point restraints beyond eight hours, which requires medical supervision. If the Shift Lieutenant observes problems, health services staff shall be contacted for further instructions.

[g.   When it is necessary to restrain an inmate for longer than eight hours, the Warden (or designee) or institution administrative duty officer shall notify the Regional Director or Regional Duty Officer by telephone.]

The notification is to be repeated for each consecutive eight hour period the restraints remain in place. Documentation as to the reasons for each placement in four-point restraints, regardless of the duration, shall be provided to the Regional Director or Regional Duty Officer on the following work day.

11. **[USE OF CHEMICAL AGENTS OR NON-LETHAL WEAPONS §552.25. The Warden may authorize the use of chemical agents or non-lethal weapons only when the situation is such that the inmate:**

    a. **Is armed and/or barricaded; or,**

    b. **Cannot be approached without danger to self or others; and,**

    c. **It is determined that a delay in bringing the situation under control would constitute a serious hazard to the inmate or others, or would result in a major disturbance or serious property damage.]**

Qualified health personnel shall be consulted prior to staff using chemical agents, pepper mace, or non-lethal weapons, unless the circumstances are such that immediate use is necessary. Whenever possible, the inmate's medical file should first be reviewed to determine whether the inmate has any diseases or condition which would be dangerously affected if the chemical agent, pepper mace, or non-lethal weapon was used. This includes, but is not limited to: asthma, emphysema, bronchitis, tuberculosis, obstructive pulmonary disease, angina pectoris, cardiac myopathy, or congestive heart failure.

Reference the Correctional Services Manual, Chapter 2, Section 207 (Page 13).

[Note: There is no #12]

13. **[MEDICAL ATTENTION IN USE OF FORCE AND APPLICATION OF RESTRAINTS INCIDENTS §552.26**

    a. **In immediate use of force situations, staff shall seek the assistance of mental health or qualified health personnel** upon gaining physical control of the inmate. When possible, staff shall seek such assistance at the onset of the violent behavior. In calculated use of force situations, the use of force team leader shall seek the guidance of qualified health personnel (based on a review of the inmate's medical record) to identify physical or mental problems. When mental health staff or qualified health personnel determine that an inmate requires continuing care, and particularly when the inmate to be restrained is pregnant, the deciding staff shall assume responsibility for the inmate's care, to include possible admission to the institution hospital, or, in the case of a pregnant inmate, restraining her in other than face down four-point restraints.

b. After any use of force or forcible application of restraints, the inmate shall be examined by qualified health personnel, and any injuries noted, immediately treated.]

If any staff involved in a use of force reports an injury, qualified health personnel should provide immediate examination and initial emergency treatment.

14. USE OF FORCE IN SPECIAL CIRCUMSTANCES. In certain extenuating circumstances, and after confrontation avoidance has failed or has proven to be impractical, staff may be forced to make a decision, such as whether to use force on a pregnant inmate or an aggressive inmate with open cuts, sores, or lesions. Special cases such as mentally ill, handicapped, or pregnant inmates, after consultation with the Clinical Director, must be carefully assessed to determine whether the situation is grave enough to require the use of physical force.

a. Pregnant Inmates. When pregnant inmates have to be restrained, necessary precautions to ensure the fetus is not harmed shall be taken. Qualified health personnel shall prescribe the necessary precautions, including decisions about the manner in which the inmate is to be restrained, whether she needs a qualified health personnel member present during the application of

213

restraints, or whether the inmate should be restrained at the institutional hospital or a local medical facility.

b.   Inmates with Wounds or Cuts. Aggressive inmates with open cuts or wounds who have attempted to harm themselves or others should be carefully approached, with staff wearing prescribed necessary protective gear. A full body shield should also be used in these instances to protect staff, if force is deemed necessary. Aggressive inmates, after being placed in restraints, should be placed in administrative detention and separated from all other inmates. Inmates of this status ordinarily shall remain in administrative detention until cleared to return to the general population by the Captain, Chief Psychologist, and the Clinical Director, and after the Warden's approval.

15.   **[DOCUMENTATION OF USE OF FORCE AND APPLICATION OF RESTRAINTS INCIDENTS §552.27. Staff shall appropriately document all incidents involving the use of force, chemical agents, or non-lethal weapons. Staff shall also document, in writing, the use of restraints on an inmate who becomes violent or displays signs of imminent violence. A copy of the report shall be placed in the inmate's central file.]**

a.   Report of Incident. A Use of Force Report (EMS-583, Attachment A) is to be prepared on the use of force, chemical agents, pepper mace, application of progressive restraints, or non-lethal weapons. This reporting requirement includes the application of progressive restraints to an inmate when the inmate is compliant with the placement into restraints. The report is to establish the identity of inmates, staff, and others involved, and is to describe the details of the incident. The report (to include mental health/medical reports) must be submitted to the Warden or designee by no later than the end of that tour of duty. A copy of the report is to be placed in the inmate's central file. Copies are also to be sent within two work days to:

(1)   Assistant Director, Correctional Programs Division;

(2)   Assistant Director, Health Services Division;

(3)   Central Office Correctional Services Administrator;

(4)   Regional Director; and,

(5)   Regional Correctional Services Administrator.

A report is not necessary for the general use of restraints (for example, the routine movement or transfer of inmates).

b.   Four-Point Restraints Report. Fifteen minute checks of inmates placed in four-point restraints shall be recorded in a bound ledger and recorded on the Special Housing Unit Report form (BP S292). Documentation of 15-minute checks shall continue until the four-point restraint placement is terminated.

During reviews of inmates' status while in four-point restraints (i.e., every two-hour review where the inmate is allowed to use the toilet facilities and his or her behavior is evaluated), each negative response by the inmate shall be documented in the bound ledger.

c.   Videotape of Use of Force Incidents. Staff shall immediately obtain and record with a video camera any use of force incident, unless it is determined that a delay in bringing the situation under control would constitute a serious hazard to the inmate, staff, or others, or would result in a major disturbance or serious property damage. This video recording shall also ordinarily include any medical examination following the application of restraints, use of chemical agents, use of pepper mace, and/or use of non-lethal weapons.

Calculated use of force shall be videotaped following the sequential guidelines presented in the Correctional Services Manual. The original videotape must be maintained and secured as evidence in the SIS Office. A copy of every calculated use of force videotape, after review by the Warden (within four work days of the incident), unless requested by the Regional Director sooner, shall be immediately provided to the Regional Director for review. The Regional Director shall forward videotapes of questionable or inappropriate cases immediately to the Assistant Director, Correctional Programs Division, Central Office, for review.

When an immediate threat to the safety of the inmate, staff or others, or to property, requires an immediate response, the staff members have an obligation to obtain a camera and begin recording the event as soon as it is feasible. Once control of the situation has been obtained, staff should record information about injuries, a description of the circumstances that gave rise to the need for immediate use of force, and the identification of the inmates, staff, and others involved.

d.   Documentation Maintenance. The Captain shall maintain all documentation, including the videotape and the original EMS 583, for a minimum of two and one-half years. A separate file shall be established on each use of force incident.

16. AFTER-ACTION REVIEW OF USE OF FORCE AND APPLICATION OF RESTRAINTS INCIDENTS. Following any incident involving the use of force, whether calculated or immediate, and the application of restraints, if applicable, the Warden, Associate Warden (responsible for Correctional Services), Captain, and the Health Services Administrator shall meet and review the incident. This review is to assess the reasonableness of the actions taken (e.g., if the force used was appropriate and in proportion to the inmate's actions).

They should gather relevant information, determine if policy was followed, and then complete a standard After-Action Report (EMS 586, Attachment B), recording the nature of their review and findings. The EMS 586 should be submitted within two working days after the inmate is removed from restraints.

a. Videotape Review. The After-Action Review Team should also review the video tape for the following:

(1) Professionalism of the Lieutenant during the Forced Cell Team technique should be evident. The Lieutenant must be in the proper Correctional Services uniform. Lieutenants should not be dressed in riot gear or wearing chains or jewelry or other ornamentation that would detract from a professional appearance. The actions of staff during a use of force situation shall be narrated by the Lieutenant supervising the situation. In addition, the Lieutenant should face the video camera and speak normally;

(2) Use of Force Team members shall wear appropriate protective gear. This ordinarily includes:

- helmet with face shield,
- coveralls,
- flack vest,
- arm and knee pads, and
- lineman gloves.

Occasionally, a plastic shield may be used to prevent staff or inmate injury. No other piece of equipment or device is authorized. Equipment not authorized includes: towels, tape, surgical mask, hosiery, etc. Each Use of Force Team member should introduce himself/herself on the video and describe his or her responsibilities.

(3) Use of Force Team members, as they enter the cell or area, must use only the amount of force necessary to subdue the inmate. If the inmate is already restrained, voluntarily submits to the placement of restraints, discontinues his or her violent behavior, etc., it may be necessary for the Use of Force Team to minimize the amount of force used.

217

The Lieutenant in charge of the Use of Force Team shall ensure only the force necessary is used, based on the nature of the situation. The Lieutenant must clearly monitor the actions of the inmate and the team members. The Lieutenant should not be actively involved in subduing the inmate, unless it is determined necessary to prevent staff or inmate injury;

(4) The application of restraints by team members must be reviewed to ensure no more pressure than necessary is applied to the inmate's thorax (chest and back), throat, head and extremities;

(5) The amount of time it takes for team members to restrain the inmate should be reviewed. If an excessive amount of time elapses; i.e., more than five minutes, and the inmate is not struggling with staff, it may be that team members are not adequately trained;

(6) Team members should not remove protective gear while inside the cell or area. Protective gear must remain on team members during the entire process;

(7) The videotape must run continuously during the entire process. If there are breaks or apparent missing sequences in the video, reviewers must question why and document the propriety of the explanation;

(8) A member of the health services staff must promptly examine the inmate after the move and the findings must be noted by that person on the videotape;

(9) When a Stun Gun, chemical agents, or pepper mace is used, the method of use must be determined. Review Team members should ensure that use of these devices was in accordance with existing policy; i.e., the Program Statements on the Use of Federal 203-A Gas Gun with Zuriel Adapter (Stun Gun) and the Correctional Services Manual;

(10) Prior to the team entering the cell, the inmate was given the opportunity to voluntarily submit to the placement of restraints. If he or she submits, then team action is ordinarily unnecessary; and,

(11) Inappropriate conversations (derogatory, demeaning, taunting, etc.) occurring between team members and the inmate, or between team members and individuals outside of the cell or area.

b. Report Completion. When this review is completed, an After-Action Review Report (EMS-586, Attachment B) shall be completed, as soon as possible, not later than two working days after the inmate has been removed from restraints. Accordingly, the length of time an inmate is kept in restraints is appropriate. This will ensure that staff having relevant information will be available and that any necessary medical follow-up can be immediately provided to ascertain the nature of any injuries involved.

The Warden or designee shall then personally attest by his or her signature that the review has taken place and that the use of force was either appropriate or inappropriate.

c. Further Investigation. The reviewers should also decide if the matter requires further investigation, and whether the incident should be referred to the Office of Internal Affairs, the Office of the Inspector General, or the FBI. If deemed appropriate, the Warden's rationale for such an assessment shall be included. Copies of this report shall be forwarded to the Assistant Director, Correctional Programs and the Regional Director.

d. Report on Restraints Use. A report is not necessary for the general use of restraints. For example, a report is not required in the routine movement or transfer of inmates.

17. TRAINING IN THE CONFRONTATION AVOIDANCE/USE OF FORCE TECHNIQUE. In order to control any potential situation involving aggressive inmates, all staff must be made aware of their responsibilities through ongoing training. At a minimum, training must cover:

- communication techniques,

- cultural diversity,

- dealing with the mentally ill,

- confrontation avoidance procedures,

- the application of restraints (progressive and hard), and

- reporting procedures.

a. Training Topics. A sufficient number of institution staff should be trained annually in both confrontation avoidance procedures and forced cell move techniques. Each staff member participating in a calculated forced cell move must have documented proof of annual training in these areas. Training should also include specific information pertaining to special situations.

b. Restraints Training. Staff should be thoroughly trained in the use of soft and hard restraints. Soft restraints can be cumbersome to apply on an inmate, if proper training is not provided. Soft restraints such as vinyl or leather restraints should be used prior to applying hard restraints. For pregnant inmates, the approved vinyl or leather restraint belt should be used instead of a metal waist chain, whenever possible, to prevent injury to the inmate or fetus.

Kathleen M. Hawk
Director

P.S. 5566.05
July 26, 1996
Attachment A, Page 1

REPORT OF INCIDENT (EMS FORM 583—MARCH 1996)

SECTION 1: GENERAL INFORMATION

INSTITUTION:

REGION:

REPORT DATE:

SUBMITTED BY:

DATE/TIME OF INCIDENT:

FBI NOTIFIED: _____YES _____ NO

USMS NOTIFIED: _____YES _____ NO

PROHIBITED ACT CODE(S):

INCIDENT REPORT NUMBER(S):

TYPE OF INCIDENT:

( ) ESCAPE OR ( )ATTEMPTED ESCAPE
[COMPLETE SECTIONS 1, 2, & 6]

( )ASSAULT, INMATE ON INMATE
[COMPLETE SECTIONS 1 & 6]

( )ASSAULT, INMATE ON STAFF
[COMPLETE SECTIONS 1 & 6]

(   )INMATE DEATH
[COMPLETE SECTIONS 1, 3, & 6]

(   )FIGHT
[COMPLETE SECTIONS 1 & 6]

(   )CELL FIRE
[COMPLETE SECTIONS 1 & 6]

(   )SELF MUTILATION
[COMPLETE SECTIONS 1 & 6]

(   )SUICIDE ATTEMPT
[COMPLETE SECTIONS 1 & 6]

(   )INTRODUCTION OF CONTRABAND
[COMPLETE SECTIONS 1 & 6]

(   )DISRUPTIVE BEHAVIOR
[COMPLETE SECTIONS 1 & 6]

(   )WEAPONS DISCHARGE
[COMPLETE SECTIONS 1, 4, & 6]

(   )USE OF FORCE
[COMPLETE SECTIONS 1, 5 & 6]

(   )MISCELLANEOUS (SPECIFY)
[COMPLETE SECTIONS 1 & 6]

WAS WEAPON USED?

IF WEAPON WAS USED, WHAT TYPE?

INMATE (S) INVOLVED
SEX CIMS MGMT INT
REG. NO. M/F RACE CITZ CATEGORY GROUP

1.

2.

3.

4.

5.

RACIAL/ETHNIC/SECURITY THREAT GROUP CONFLICT:

INMATE NAME REG. NO. GROUP SUSPECT/CONFIRMED:

1.

2.

3.

STAFF INJURIES: (   )YES (   )NO

INMATE INJURIES: (   )YES (   )NO

IF MEDICAL TREATMENT REQUIRED BY EITHER STAFF OR INMATES, LIST NAMES, INJURIES, TREATMENT AND NAME OF MEDICAL STAFF PRESENT PRIOR TO OR DURING INCIDENT:

SECTION 2: ESCAPE OR ATTEMPTED ESCAPE

ESCAPE OR ATTEMPTED ESCAPE OCCURRED FROM:

____ INSIDE PERIMETER   ____ OUTSIDE PERIMETER

____ ESCORTED TRIP

____ FURLOUGH (SOCIAL/LEGAL/MEDICAL)

____ FURLOUGH (INSTITUTION TO INSTITUTION)

____ FURLOUGH (INSTITUTION TO COMMUNITY
CONFINEMENT CENTER)

____ OTHER (SPECIFY):

SECTION 3: INMATE DEATH

INMATE DEATH (LOCATION):

CAUSE OF DEATH:

INVESTIGATIVE STEPS BEING TAKEN, IF NECESSARY:

CITIZENSHIP: ____ USA ____ OTHER.
IF ALIEN, HAVE CONSULAR AND IMMIGRATION OFFICE
BEEN NOTIFIED? (   ) YES (   ) NO

SURVIVOR / DESIGNEE (   ) HAS (   ) HAS NOT BEEN NOTIFIED

NAME AND ADDRESS OF SURVIVOR OR DESIGNEE:

MEDICAL COMMENTS:

SECTION 4: WEAPONS DISCHARGE

NAME OF EMPLOYEE:

POST ASSIGNMENT:

TYPE OF WEAPON:

DISCHARGE WAS: (   ) ACCIDENTAL (   ) LINE OF DUTY

NUMBER OF ROUNDS FIRED:

REGIONAL OFFICE (   ) WAS (   ) WAS NOT NOTIFIED.

CAPTAIN'S ANALYSIS AND DAMAGE REPORT:

DAMAGE ESTIMATE: $

TRAINING NEEDS INDICATED: (   )YES (   ) NO.
IF YES, EXPLAIN:

SECTION 5: USE OF FORCE/RESTRAINTS/CHEMICAL AGENTS/ NON-LETHAL WEAPONS

USE OF FORCE CLASSIFICATION:
(   ) EMERGENCY, UNPLANNED USE OF FORCE
(   ) CALCULATED, PLANNED USE OF FORCE

RESTRAINT EQUIPMENT USED:
(   ) NONE (   ) SOFT (   ) HARD

RESTRAINT METHOD USED:

(   )AMBULATORY (   )2-POINT (   )4-POINT

DATE/TIME PLACED IN RESTRAINTS:

USE OF RESTRAINTS AUTHORIZED BY:

OTHER EQUIPMENT USED:

LIST OF OTHER STAFF SUBMITTING

CHEMICAL AGENTS (TYPE, QUANTITY)

MEMOS EXCLUDING PRINCIPLE STAFF:
(   ) STUN GUN (RANGE, # OF ROUNDS)
(   ) BATON
(   ) SHIELD
(   ) MAG-LIGHT
(   ) OTHER: (DESCRIBE)

REASON FOR USE OF FORCE:
(   ) CONFRONTATION AVOIDANCE PROVED INEFFECTIVE
(   ) BECAME VIOLENT AND/OR ASSAULTIVE
(   ) DISPLAYED SIGNS OF IMMINENT VIOLENCE
(   ) DESTROYING PROPERTY
(   ) ATTEMPTED SUICIDE
(   ) INFLICTED WOUNDS ON SELF/OTHERS
(   ) ENFORCEMENT OF INSTITUTION REGULATIONS
(   ) PREVENTION OF A CRIME
(   ) APPREHENSION OF ONE WHO HAS COMMITTED A CRIME
(   ) OTHER: (SPECIFY)

LIST FULL NAME OF ALL PRINCIPLE STAFF INVOLVED IN
INCIDENT:

CONFRONTATION AVOIDANCE (LIST NAME AND TITLE)

1.

2.

3.

4.

5.

6.

FORCE CELL TEAM MEMBERS, IF USED (LIST NAME
AND TITLE):

1.

2.

3.

4.

5.

6.

WAS THE INCIDENT VIDEOTAPED SEQUENTIALLY AS OUT-
LINED IN THE CORRECTIONAL SERVICES MANUAL? IF NO,
EXPLAIN WHY NOT, AND INDICATE AT WHAT POINT TAPING
DID BEGIN.

(   ) YES

(   ) NO

INDICATE TAPE ECN (EVIDENCE CONTROL NUMBER):

SECTION 6: DESCRIPTION OF INCIDENT

DESCRIPTION OF INCIDENT (IF USE OF FORCE, INCLUDE DETAILS, SUCH AS NAME OF THE SUPERVISOR APPLYING THE CHEMICAL AGENT AND/OR RESTRAINTS, REASONS FOR USE OF HARD RESTRAINTS INSTEAD OF SOFT RESTRAINTS, ETC.)

ROUTING: REGION CEO; REGION CORR SVC; BOP CEO; BOP CORR SVC; BOP MED SVC

FILE: CAPTAIN; INMATE CENTRAL FILE

P.S. 5566.05
July 25, 1996
Attachment B, Page 1

AFTER-ACTION REVIEW REPORT
USE OF FORCE/RESTRAINTS/CHEMICAL AGENTS/
NON-LETHAL WEAPONS
(EMS FORM 586)

INSTITUTION:

REGION:

REPORT DATE:

SUBMITTED BY:

DATE/TIME OF INCIDENT:

INCIDENT LOCATION (EXAMPLE: SHU):

PROHIBITED ACT CODE(S):

INCIDENT REPORT NUMBER(S):

USE OF FORCE CLASSIFICATION:
(   ) EMERGENCY, UNPLANNED USE OF FORCE
(   ) CALCULATED, PLANNED USE OF FORCE

USE OF RESTRAINTS CLASSIFICATION:
(   ) NONE USED
(   ) BRIEF, EMERGENCY USE WHILE UNDER SUPERVISION/
      ESCORT
(   ) ONGOING USE

DATE/TIME PLACED IN RESTRAINTS:

DATE/TIME RELEASED FROM RESTRAINTS:

DATE/TIMES REGIONAL DIRECTOR NOTIFIED OF EACH
ADDITIONAL 8 HOUR TIME PERIOD:

INMATES INVOLVED
REG. NO. SEX M/F RACE* CITIZENSHIP* CIMS CATE-
GORY**

1)

2)

3)

NAMES OF PARTICIPANTS IN AFTER-ACTION REVIEW:
(MUST INCLUDE THE WARDEN OR ACTING WARDEN, ASSO-
CIATE WARDEN FOR CORRECTIONAL SERVICES, CAPTAIN,
AND A MEMBER OF THE MEDICAL STAFF)

INDICATE THE ITEMS REVIEWED:

(   ) CONFRONTATION AVOIDANCE MEASURES

(   ) VIDEO TAPE OF THE INCIDENT

(   ) STAFF MEMOS

---

*CODES:
RACE = W/WHITE, B/BLACK, A/ASIAN, I/AMERICAN INDIAN
CITZ = SENTRY CITIZENSHIP, SUCH AS: CU/CUBA, CO/COLOMBIA,
        MX/MEXICO, JM/JAMAICA, HA/HAITI, ETC.

**CIMS CATEGORIES:
        SCA, STATE, SEPARATION, DISR GROUP, OTHER (SPECIF)

(   ) MEDICAL REPORTS OF EXAMINATION AND INJURIES

(   ) SUPERVISOR'S REPORT

(   ) TYPE OF RESTRAINTS USED

(   ) METHOD OF RESTRAINT

(   ) OTHER: (SPECIFY)

Appendix C

Survey Instrument

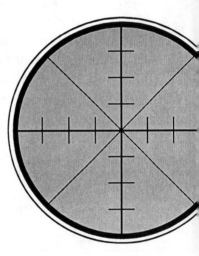

Name of Department/Facility:

_____

AMERICAN CORRECTIONAL ASSOCIATION USE-OF-FORCE SURVEY

This survey should be filled out by the person in your department *best suited* to answer questions about use of force policies. It is important for us to obtain this information from you. It should take about 20 minutes to complete the survey. Please fill out the survey as completely and accurately as possible, and return the completed survey to the American Correctional Association by February 2, 1998. Please feel free to use additional paper or use the last page for any lengthy comments.

PLEASE ATTACH ANY RELEVANT INFORMATION AND MATERIAL, SUCH AS WRITTEN USE-OF-FORCE POLICIES AND PROCEDURES. THIS IS VERY IMPORTANT!

1. Does your department have a <u>written</u> use-of-force policy?

_____ YES   _____ NO

(PLEASE ENCLOSE A COPY OF THE USE-OF-FORCE POLICY AND ANY OTHER DOCUMENTS CONCERNING USE OF FORCE)

2. Does your department's use-of-force policy include <u>specialized applications of force</u> (such as four-point restraints)?

_____ YES   _____ NO   _____ DON'T KNOW

3. Does your department's use-of-force policy include <u>specialized restraint techniques</u> (such as restraint chairs)?

_____ YES   _____ NO   _____ DON'T KNOW

4. Does your department's use-of-force policy include specialized confinement conditions (such as "strip cells")?

____ YES   ____ NO   ____ DON'T KNOW

5. How does your department <u>define</u> the use of force?

6. How does your department <u>monitor</u> the use of force?

7. Are staff required to prepare a <u>written report</u> for all use-of-force incidents?

____ YES   ____ NO   ____ DON'T KNOW

If YES, is a prepared form provided?

____ YES   ____ NO   ____ DON'T KNOW

(IF YES, PLEASE ENCLOSE A COPY OF THE FORM)

If YES, what information is requested?

8. Is there an <u>administrative review process</u> in place for use-of-force incidents?

____ YES   ____ NO   ____ DON'T KNOW

If YES, what is the job title of the person who conducts the review?

9. Are all use-of-force incidents subject to administrative review?

____ YES   ____ NO   ____ DON'T KNOW

10. Are use-of-force incidents reported to the central administration or some central authority for the department?

_____ YES _____ NO _____ DON'T KNOW

11. Does your administrative review process require a <u>formal declaration in writing</u> as to whether the type and extent of force used in an incident was appropriate?

_____ YES _____ NO _____ DON'T KNOW

12. What criteria determines whether or not a use-of-force incident is reviewed?

13. Does the administrative review include an <u>interview</u> with all staff who are involved or are witnesses to the use-of-force incident?

_____ YES _____ NO _____ DON'T KNOW

14. How many administrative levels participate in the review? <u>Check all that apply</u>.

_____ shift commander _____ regional staff

_____ managers _____ central office staff

_____ superintendents _____ other (please specify):

15. How often are use-of-force policies <u>reviewed and/or updated</u> in your department?

_____ never _____ after major incident

_____ daily _____ don't know

_____ annual training _____ other (please specify):

_____ special session

16. When is the use-of-force policy <u>reviewed with line officers</u>?

_____ never   _____ after major incident

_____ daily   _____ don't know

_____ annual training   _____ other (please specify):

_____ special session

17. Are there clear policies outlining when <u>escalation of force</u> is authorized?

_____ YES   _____ NO   _____ DON'T KNOW

18. What <u>equipment</u> does your department have for situations involving use of force?

_____ chemical agents   _____ firearms

_____ stun guns   _____ body armor

_____ shields   _____ other (please specify):

19. Does your department provide formal training for each type of use-of-force <u>equipment</u>?

_____ YES   _____ NO   _____ DON'T KNOW

20. Does your department provide formal training on use-of-force <u>techniques</u>?

_____ YES   _____ NO   _____ DON'T KNOW

21. Does your department provide formal training on use-of-force *philosophy* (such as attitude, professionalism, implications of use of force on inmate/staff relations)?

_____ YES   _____ NO   _____ DON'T KNOW

22. How many hours of required, formal <u>self-defense training</u> does your department provide?

_____ 0   _____ 21-30

_____ 1-10   _____ 31-40

_____ 11-20   _____ 41+

23. What types of <u>self-defense training</u> does your department provide?

_____ aikido   _____ use of chemical agents

_____ firearms   _____ conflict resolution

_____ restraint techniques   _____ other (please specify):

24. What types of formal <u>crisis intervention training</u> does your department provide?

25. What types of formal training in handling <u>aggressive inmates</u> does your department provide?

26. What types of <u>control/restraint techniques</u> are <u>NOT PERMITTED</u> in your department? Please list all that are prohibited.

27. Where do use-of-force incidents <u>most often</u> occur in institutions within your department?

_____ housing area   _____ hospital area

_____ work area   _____ don't know

_____ recreation area   _____ eating area

_____ other (please specify)

28. How many times did inmates <u>physically attack staff</u> in the past year in your department? If the exact number is known, please write it in the space provided:

_____ 0   _____ 76-100

_____ 1-25   _____ 101-125

_____ 26-50   _____ 126-150

_____ 51-75   _____ 151+   _____

29. How many times did inmates <u>use a weapon on staff</u> in the past year in your department? If the exact number is known, please write it in the space provided:

_____ 0   _____ 76-100

_____ 1-25   _____ 101-125

_____ 26-50   _____ 126-150

_____ 51-75   _____ 151+   _____

30. How many use-of-force incidents <u>occurred</u> in your department in the last year? If the exact number is known, please write it in the space provided:

_____ 0   _____ 76-100

_____ 1-25   _____ 101-125

_____ 26-50   _____ 126-150

_____ 51-75   _____ 151+   _____

31. Of these use-of-force incidents, how many involved <u>excessive force</u>? If the exact number is known, please write it in the space provided:

_____ 0   _____ 76-100

_____ 1-25   _____ 101-125

_____ 26-50   _____ 126-150

_____ 51-75   _____ 151+   _____

32. Of those incidents involving excessive use of force, how many resulted in some form of <u>disciplinary action</u> for the officer(s) involved? If the exact number is known, please write it in the space provided:

_____ 0	_____ 76-100
_____ 1-25	_____ 101-125
_____ 26-50	_____ 126-150
_____ 51-75	_____ 151+ _____

33. Do you have enough staff to provide <u>adequate security</u> in all of your institutions?

_____ YES   _____ NO   _____ DON'T KNOW

34. What percentage of your security posts are commonly <u>closed due to staffing shortages</u>?

_____ 0%	_____ 31-40%
_____ 1-10%	_____ 41-50%
_____ 11-20%	_____ 51%+
_____ 21-30%	_____ don't know

35. Does your department routinely use <u>videotape</u> in use of force situations?

_____ YES   _____ NO   _____ DON'T KNOW

36. Does your department have a <u>special unit</u> for use-of-force incidents (such as a cell extraction team)?

_____ YES   _____ NO   _____ DON'T KNOW

37. How many <u>inmate lawsuits</u> alleging unlawful use of force are <u>currently pending</u> against your department? If the exact number is known, please write it in the space provided:

_____ 0   _____ 31-40

_____ 1-10   _____ 41-50

_____ 11-20   _____ 51+

_____ 21-30   _____ don't know   _____

38. Have you noticed any <u>changes in inmate lawsuits</u> alleging unlawful use of force since Congress passed the Prison Litigation Reform Act (PLRA) in 1996?

_____ YES   _____ NO   _____ DON'T KNOW

If YES, Please Explain:

39. Does your department have <u>high security units</u> for violent and disruptive inmates?

_____ YES   _____ NO   _____ DON'T KNOW

If YES, <u>how many</u> inmates are confined in these units?

What <u>percentage</u> of the department's total inmate population is housed in these units?

40. What future plans, if any, does your department have for creating high security units for violent and disruptive inmates?

Please feel free to include any additional comments or information that you may have regarding use of force policies and procedures.

PLEASE REMEMBER TO SEND A COPY OF ANY MATERIAL THAT YOUR DEPARTMENT HAS WHICH IS RELATED TO USE OF FORCE. THIS INCLUDES USE-OF-FORCE POLICIES, TRAINING MATERIAL, REPORT FORMS, AND ANYTHING ELSE RELATED TO THE SUBJECT.

Please return the completed survey to the ACA by February 2, 1998, in the enclosed self-addressed stamped envelope. Please ship all other material under separate cover to the same address, listed below:

> American Correctional Association
> 4380 Forbes Boulevard
> Lanham, MD 20706
> Attn: Alice Fins/Use-of-Force Survey

THANK YOU FOR YOUR TIME AND INPUT.

Appendix D

Sample Use-of-Force Incident Review Memo

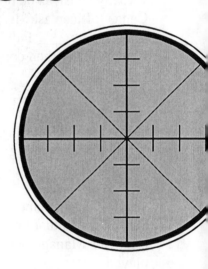

<u>MEMORANDUM</u>

DATE: April 15, 1999

TO: _____ _____, Warden

FROM: _____ _____, Administrative Officer

SUBJECT: Use-of-Force Investigation

               _____, _____ 00000 - March 24, 1999

REVIEW OF INCIDENT

The following investigation report is the result of a review of all incident/information reports, video tapes, and interviews with staff who were involved in the incident which occurred on March 24, 1999, resulting in use of force against inmate _____ #00000.

At approximately 3:02 p.m. on March 24, 1999, inmate _____ contacted the E Pod Control Center via the intercom. Inmate _____ was verbally abusive and demanded that he talk to the Lieutenant. The Control Center officer asked inmate _____ what this was in regard to and inmate _____ indicated that it was none of his business. The Control Center officer then contacted the Pod Lieutenant.

At approximately 3:30 p.m., while staff were passing out Canteen slips in day hall 8, inmate _____ threatened staff and was verbally abusive because he did not get any mail that day. Inmate _____ then began kicking and banging on his cell door, while continuing to verbally abuse staff.

The Pod Lieutenant contacted the CSP Shift Commander and appraised her of the situation. It was decided to activate inmate _____'s Behavior Management Plan because of the specific behavior being displayed. Lt. _____, along with two (2) other staff, then responded to inmate _____'s cell and informed him that he was being placed on his Behavior Management Plan due to his abusive and threatening behavior. Inmate _____ was ordered to cuff up so that he could be brought into compliance with the Behavior Management Plan. Inmate _____ refused to comply with all orders. The Pod Lieutenant then contacted the Shift Commander and informed her that inmate was refusing to cuff up.

The Shift Commander then responded to inmate _____'s cell and inmate _____ told her he had gone off because he had not received any mail. The Shift Commander explained to inmate _____ that he needed to be appropriate with staff and not verbally abusive and threatening. She further explained that this type of behavior was identified in his Behavior Management Plan and that is the reason he was being placed on his Behavior Management Plan. Inmate _____ refused to comply with the Shift Commander's orders to cuff up. The Shift Commander contacted the CSP Duty Officer and informed her of the situation. The Shift Commander was given authorization to activate the forced cell entry team. The team was assembled, briefed, and then proceeded to E Pod. Inmate _____ had jammed his cell door and thus the door had to be cleared by maintenance staff. Inmate _____ also was observed smearing feces from the toilet on himself and on the inside of the cell.

The cell extraction team entered day hall 8 at approximately 7:02 p.m. Inmate _____ was ordered to come to the door and cuff up. Inmate _____ did comply with the order, was cuffed, and then ordered to kneel down in the middle of the cell floor facing the rear wall. Inmate _____ did comply with the orders. The team then entered the cell and applied the leg restraints. Inmate _____ was taken to the E Pod hallway where he was strip searched and examined by medical staff. Inmate _____ was then placed on a gurney and taken to the Intake/Orientation area where he was placed in the shower. At that point inmate _____ was placed in holding cell G137.

FINDINGS

On March 24, 1999, at approximately 3:02 p.m., inmate _____ contacted the E Pod Control Center via the cell intercom. He told the Control Center officer, CO _____, "I want to talk to the fucking Lieutenant or I'm going off." CO _____ asked inmate _____ what this was regarding and inmate _____ replied, "It's none of your mother-fucking business. Get the Lieutenant now or I'm going off." CO _____ then contacted the Pod Lieutenant, _____.

At approximately 3:30 p.m., while staff were passing out Canteen slips in day hall E8, inmate _____ became verbally abusive and threatening to staff because he didn't get any mail that day. CO _____ indicated to inmate _____ that he had no control over his mail, but that he (inmate) would get mail if there was mail to give him. Inmate _____ then began kicking and banging on his cell door, yelling obscenities. Inmate _____ then stated to CO _____, "I will kick your ass. Go ahead and open the door."

Lt. _____ contacted the CSP Shift Commander, Capt. _____, and informed her of the situation. The decision was made to place inmate _____ on his Behavior Management Plan due to the specific behavior being displayed. Lt. _____, along with two (2) escort staff (_____ and _____), responded to inmate _____'s cell and informed him that he was being placed on his Behavior Management Plan due to the abusive and threatening behavior. In order that inmate _____ be brought into compliance with his Behavior Management Plan, he was ordered to cuff up so that he could be removed from the cell. Inmate _____ refused to comply with any of the orders to cuff up.

At approximately 3:59 p.m. Lt. _____ notified Capt. _____ that inmate _____ had refused to cuff up. It should be noted at this point that as a result of inmate _____'s verbally abusive and threatening behavior, he was not fed the evening meal.

At approximately 6:23 p.m. Capt. _____ responded to inmate _____'s cell. Inmate _____ indicated to her that he had gone off because he had not received any mail. Capt. _____ reiterated the fact that inmate _____ was being placed on his Behavior Management Plan due to his verbally abusive and threatening behavior. Capt. _____ at that point ordered inmate _____ to cuff up. Inmate _____ again refused to comply with the order. Capt. _____ explained that if he continued to refuse, she would be forced to utilize the cell extraction team to bring him into compliance. Inmate _____ continued to refuse to cuff up. Capt. ____ then contacted the CSP Duty Officer, _____ and appraised her of the situation. At approximately 6:30 p.m. Capt. _____ was given authorization to activate the forced cell entry team. The team was assembled, briefed, and consisted of:

Team Member #1:   _____

Team Member #2:   _____

Team Member #3:   _____

Team Member #4: _____

Team Member #5: _____

Video Camera Operator: _____

CSP Medical Staff: _____

At approximately 7:18 p.m. Lt. _____, _____ (CSP Maintenance), and CO _____ entered day hall 8 to check on the condition of inmate _____'s cell. Inmate _____ had jammed the cell door with pencils and library books. Maintenance was able to clear the door with the door rail tool. Inmate _____ was observed taking feces out of the toilet and smearing it on the cell window and himself. Kitty litter was thrown under the cell door in order to absorb the moisture and to create a less slippery condition. The cell extraction team entered the day hall at approximately 7:21 p.m. The team point man, CO _____, gave inmate _____ verbal orders to, "Come to the door and cuff up!" Inmate _____ did comply with the order. Inmate _____ was then ordered to, "Kneel in the middle of the floor facing the rear of the cell." Inmate _____ did comply with the order. The team then entered the cell and applied the leg restraints. Inmate _____ agreed to continue to cooperate with the team and thus was walked out of the cell. He was escorted to the E Pod hallway area where he was strip searched and examined by medical staff. Nurse _____ noted: "Officers called medical to E Pod for a cell extraction on inmate _____. I did a full head-to-toe assessment on the inmate in the hallway of E Pod. I asked him if he had any medical needs at this time, and he declined."

Inmate _____ was then placed on a gurney and taken down to the Intake/Orientation area where he was placed in the shower. The reason inmate _____ was taken down to the Intake area on the gurney was because he was covered with feces. After showering inmate _____ was placed in holding cell G137.

A contact with Medical Services this date, April 15, 1999, indicates that there has been no subsequent injury or complaint of injury as a result of this use of force.

Based on this investigation, it is my determination that use of force in this situation was justified and not excessive.

RECOMMENDATIONS

Although the cell extraction was very passive, the team was placed in a very unenviable position, considering that inmate _____ had smeared feces all over himself. The team should be commended for a job well done. All staff involved should be commended for their professionalism.

One aspect of this incident that needs to be addressed, which is not directly related to the use of force, revolves around the fact that inmate _____ was not fed his evening meal because of his verbally abusive and threatening behavior. This is unacceptable. Food is not to be used as punishment in a correctional setting. Feeding inmate _____ in a styrofoam tray may have been more appropriate. The only time staff can withhold an inmate's meal is if the inmate has refused to turn in the meal trays from the previous meal.

DB/ _____

xc:

Appendix E

Sample Use-of-Force Report

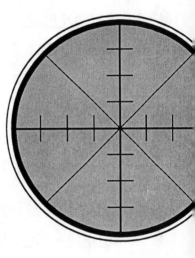

DC FORM 300-16B (01/98) *TYPE OR PRINT ONLY!*

DEPARTMENT OF CORRECTIONS

USE-OF-FORCE REPORT

DATE/TIME OF INCIDENT:

1. <u>SHIFT COMMANDER INFORMATION</u>:

EMPLOYEE NAME:

EMPLOYEE RANK:

2. <u>IDENTIFICATION OF SUBJECT</u>:

SUBJECT NAME (LAST, FIRST, MI):

DOC NUMBER: SEX, FACILITY/UNIT

EXACT LOCATION OF INCIDENT:

3. <u>REASON FOR THE USE OF FORCE</u>:

(   ) NECESSARY TO EFFECT ARREST

(   ) NECESSARY TO PREVENT PROPERTY DAMAGE

(   ) NECESSARY TO DEFEND REPORTING OFFICER

(   ) PREVENT OFFENDER FROM INFLICTING SELF-INJURY

(   ) NECESSARY TO PREVENT ESCAPE

(   ) OTHER

4. <u>MEDICAL EXAMINATION</u>:

DATE:

TIME:

LOCATION OF MEDICAL EXAM:

NAME OF ATTENDING MEDICAL STAFF:

(   ) CHECK HERE IF SUBJECT REFUSED TO ALLOW MEDICAL
STAFF EXAMINATION:

5. <u>SUBJECT'S ACTIONS</u>:

A. AT THE TIME OF THE INCIDENT WAS THE SUBJECT:

(   ) SUSPECT UNDER THE INFLUENCE OF ALCOHOL

(   ) SUSPECT UNDER THE INFLUENCE OF CHEMICAL

(   ) DRUG SUSPECTED

(   ) MENTAL DISORDER

B. LEVEL OF RESISTANCE BY SUBJECT (EXPLAIN):

PSYCHOLOGICAL INTIMIDATION:

VERBAL THREATS:

PASSIVE RESISTANCE:

DEFENSIVE RESISTANCE:

ACTIVE AGGRESSION:

AGGRAVATED ACTIVE AGGRESSION/TYPE OF WEAPON:

6. <u>LEVEL OF CONTROL EFFECTED BY EMPLOYEES</u>:

A. LEVEL OF CONTROL EFFECTED:

(   ) VERBAL DIRECTION—COMMANDS GIVEN:

B. TYPE OF EMPTY HAND CONTROL:

(   ) STRENGTH TECHNIQUES:

JOINT LOCKS:

(   ) PRESSURE POINTS/LOCATION:

(   ) HAND STRIKE/LOCATION:

(   ) LEG/FOOT STRIKE/LOCATION:

(   ) NECK RESTRAINT/LEVEL USED:

C. SOFT INTERMEDIATE CONTROL/TYPE:

(   ) OLEORESIN CAPSICUM (OC)/LOCATION OF USE:

(   ) ELECTRONIC RESTRAINING DEVICE/TYPE/LOCATION:

D. HARD INTERMEDIATE CONTROL/TYPE:

(   ) CHEMICAL AGENTS/TYPE/LOCATION OF USE:

(   ) INTACT WEAPON/TYPE/LOCATION OF STRIKE:

E. LETHAL ENCOUNTER/WEAPON USED:

PRESENTED: (   ) YES (   ) NO

LOW READY (   ) HIGH READY (   )

DISCHARGED: (   ) YES (   ) NO

TYPE OF WEAPON? NUMBER OF ROUNDS FIRED?

F. ADDITIONAL COMMENTS:

7. EVIDENCE:

DESCRIBE EVIDENCE OBTAINED AND DISPOSITION INCLUD-ING PHOTOS/ VIDEOS:

8. EMPLOYEE COMPLAINT OF INJURY:

NAMES:

9. ACCIDENTAL DISCHARGE OF FIREARM: (DESCRIBE IN NARRATIVE SECTION)

(   ) YES (   ) NO

10. <u>NAMES/ASSIGNMENT OF OTHER STAFF INVOLVED</u>:

NAME ASSIGNMENT/TEAM MEMBER NUMBER

11. <u>NAMES/DOC NUMBERS OF OTHER INVOLVED OFFENDERS</u>:

NAME DOC NUMBER

12. <u>SHIFT COMMANDER'S SUMMARY</u>:
(CONTINUE ON BACK, IF NECESSARY)

13. <u>AUTHENTICATION</u>:

SIGNATURE:

SHIFT COMMANDER

DATE/TIME OF REPORT:

14. <u>ADMINISTRATIVE HEAD DETERMINATION</u>:

A. WHAT TYPE OF FORCE WAS USED?

B. WAS THE TYPE OF FORCE SELECTED, JUSTIFIED AND APPROPRIATE?

(   ) YES (   ) NO

C. WAS THE AMOUNT OF FORCE APPLIED APPROPRIATE?

(   ) YES (   ) NO

COMMENTS:

ADMINISTRATIVE HEAD SIGNATURE:

DATE:

Appendix E: Sample Use-of-Force Report

Original: Administrative Head

Copies: Executive Director
          Deputy Director of Correctional Services
          Regional Director
          Inspector General

Index

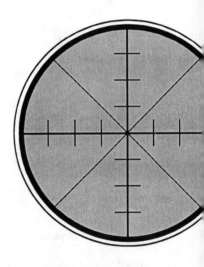

Index

identification, 162
shooting at, 162–63
Allegations against staff, 179
Ambulatory restraints, 209. *See also* Restraints
American Correctional Association (ACA)
created and promulgated professional standards, 2
model policies on use of force, 8
Standards for Correctional Institutions (1966), 20
standards for operating jails and prisons (1977), 21
standards on use of force, 60, 125–28
use of force national survey sponsored by, 39–41
use of force survey instrument, 233–42
Ammunition, 89, 132
Amount of force courts defined as proper, 25
Angina pectoris, 212
Appropriate force, 204
Archambeault and Archambeault (1982) on definition of policy, 95–96
Arkansas
allowed inmates to be whipped until 1965, 26
prison scandal, 19
used corporal punishment until the 1960s, 17
Armed inmate and use of chemical agents or nonlethal weapons, 212
Armed posts specification, 174
Armory
items and conditions of use authorization, 134
chemical agents in, 185
Arsenal sergeant responsibilities for electronic restraining devices, 152
Artery holds prohibited, 65
Assaultive inmates, younger than nonassaultive inmates, 6
Assaults
factors associated with, 6
inmate acting alone is cause of most, 6
on staff, 5, 53, 54-55
triggered by officers doing their job, 7

with a weapon, 55
Asthma, 212
Atherton, Eugene, biographic abstract, 258
Attacks. *See* Assaults
Attica prison riot focused public attention on prisons, 20
Auburn Prison in New York, 16
Authorization for the use of force
conditions permitting, 143
report, 144
restraints as a means of control, 136–37

B

Barricaded inmate and use of chemical agents or nonlethal force, 212
Baton, 66, 168, 175
active counter measures as, 170
less-than-lethal force weapon, 33
use of, 138, 175
Beanbags use, 177
Beccaria's theory of the relationship between punishment and crime, 16
Beds and restraints, 210
Best force option use, 86
Blankets, prohibited use, 205
Blood and body secretions, 208–209
Body armor
institutional policies on use of, 45–46
new and better types, 89
for work with inmates with wounds or cuts, 214
Body fluids
procedure upon spilling, 208–09
transmittal of disease, 72
Breaks in videotapes, 218
Bronchitis, 212
Building searches, 75
Bureau of Prisons. *See* Federal Bureau of Prisons
Burnout history as potential for excessive use of force, 81

C

Calculated use of force and/or application of restraints, 168, 201–02

Control center
  arsenal in, 152
  chemical agents in, 185
Conversations, inappropriate, 219
Cooper v. Pate (1964), 19
Corporal punishment, 14–16, 25
  Arkansas used until the 1960s, 17
  considered inappropriate in correctional
    institutions, 26
  definition, 17
  forbid use of, 143
  rejected by courts as legitimate in prison,
    17
Correctional goals, 17
Correctional officers
  liability of, 2, 34
  personnel lawfully using force against
    inmates, 26
  presence of, as lowest level of nonphysical
    force, 63–64
  questions to ask when breaking up
    inmate fight, 67–68
  and reasonable force, 2
  role of, 4–7
Correctional law, recommended works on,
  24
Correctional Services Manual, 218
Correctional standards, purpose of, 11; *see
    also* American Correctional Standards
    "Declaration of Principles", 20
  use of force policies vary in specificity, 8
Corrections, public awareness of, 2
Corrections departments
  challenges of, 1
  operating policies of, 2
Cothran, Larry, viii
Counselors, in calculated use of force, 202,
  207
Coveralls, 217
CPR or first aid administration, 73
Crime prevention permitting active counter
  measures without prior approval, 172
Criminal activity, use of force to prevent, 28,
  204
Criminal and civil proceedings resulting
  from excessive use of force, 78

"Cruel and unusual" punishment, 24–26.
    See also Eighth Amendment
CS, 168. *See also* Orthochlorbenzalmalononi-
    trile; Chemical agents
  agent, 154
  use of gas, 184
  hard intermediate control devices, 66
  only used in buildings as last resort, 154
Cuffing with resistance, 65
Cultural diversity training, 220
Culture of terror, 81
Czerniak, Stan, viii

D

Damage to property prevention, 143
Dangerous felon, Supreme Court ruling
  involving apprehension of, 28
Deadly force, 168
  as level of force, 171–74
  means of regaining order in California, 29
  never justified to prevent property
    damage, 28
  to prevent escape from correctional
    facilities, 28, 33
  use of less than, 33
  use of, 32–33
  Walker's (1996) review of cases dealing
    with use of, 33
  when used, 68, 69, 75, 135, 180
Death penalty, 14–15, 25
Decision factors
  chemical agents, 136
"Declaration of Principles" corrections
  standard, 20
Decontamination
  after the use of chemical agent, 157–58,
    186, 190
  chemical agents, 136
  training in procedures of, 188
Defense of others in use of force, 27, 172
Definitions of terms on use-of-force
  policies, 85
Delaware allowed whipping in prisons until
  1954, 17
Deliberate indifference, 26, 34, 92
  administrators can be charged with, 28
  Court declined to use standard of, 30

Index

Handicapped inmates and use of force, 213–14
Handheld device, electronic restraint device as, 66
Hands-off policy, 13, 19, 30
    of judiciary out of concern for a separation of powers, 18
    result of erosion of, 92
Hands-on physical force, 148
Hanson and Daley (1995) on Section 1983 cases filed by inmate plaintiffs, 92
Hard restraints, 194, 206
Harm
    correctional officers may use force to prevent greater, 27–28
    legal remedies for, 34
Harassment or punishment, physical force shall not be used for, 134
Health personnel; *See also* Medical attention and use of chemical agents, 212
    visits to restrained prisoner, 211, 218
Helicopter assisted escapes/assaults, 161–65
Helmets, 88
    with face shields, 208, 217
Hemmens, Craig, biographic abstract for, 257–58
High-intensity water stream delivery of control chemicals, 89
History of use of force in corrections, 13–21
HIV positive inmates, procedures for, 208
Hog-tying prohibited, 206
Hosiery prohibited usage, 205, 217
Housing areas, location of most serious assaults on correctional officers, 5
Houston (1995) on definition of policy, 96
Hudson v. McMillan (1992), 31–32, 92–93

I

Immediate use of force, 169, 201
Immunity, 36–37
Implementation
    definition of, 99
    of use-of-force policy, 99–100
"Incapacitation" as correctional goal, 17
Incarceration, nature of, 2
In-cell restraint, 132, 136–37

Incident review memo sample, 243–48
Indoor use of chemical agents, 184
Inexperienced officers most likely to be assaulted, 6
Inflammatory agent, 155, 168. *See also* Oleoresin Capsicum (OC)
Inflammatory agents use, 177
Information sheet for use of force, 181
Infrared vision for towers and perimeter vehicles, 89
Injury required for federal action in use of force, 31–32
Inmate(s)
    abuse reports, 146–47
    aggressive, 174–75
    assaults, 5, 6, 53–55
    changes in rights of, 2
    death report, 224
    fight, questions to ask when, 67
    lawsuits, 25, 34, 57–58, 94–95
        as primary forces for change in correctional policies and procedures, 2
        function of size rather than problems, 58
    likely to cause death or serious physical injury, 175
    suing prison officials, 19
    tracking, 75
    uncooperative, 174
    violence relevant factors, 4
    with wounds or cuts, 214
Institutional policies, role of, 9–11
Institutional regulations, enforcement of, 204
Intermediate control devices [soft/hard] as level of physical force, 66–68
Interview
    as administrative oversight of use-of-force incidents, 48
    with officer(s) involved in use of force importance, 83
Intoxicated individuals, use of electronic restraining devices on, 150
Investigation, report of, 145–46
Irritant agent, 155. *See also* CS
Ispra Projecto Jet, 66

261

Index

Public contact with offender during transport, 196–97
Punishment
  chemical agents never used on inmate, 154
  cruel and unusual court tests, 25
  evolution over the last few centuries, 17
  force on inmate, 204
  in excess of reasonable level force must never be used, 62
  means of achieving a larger goal, 16

Q
Quasijudicial immunity, 37

R
Race grouping of inmates as danger sign, 81
Radio communication systems for tactical convenience, 88
Reactive approach to inmate litigation, 2
"Reasonable" force, 3, 29–30
  basic standard, 115
  conditions allowed for prison officials, 25
  definition of, 7–8
  justified by correctional personnel to maintain security, 32
"Reasonable person" standard, 30
Religious beliefs as a reason for inmate litigation, 2
Removal of protective gear within cell or area, 218
Reporting
  completion of reports, 219
  to central authority as oversight of use-of-force incidents, 48
  on force used, 166
  of incident, 214–15, 221–28
  and record keeping, 139
  requirements, 178–79
  on restraints use, 219
Report review for serious incident review, 140
Research essential to keep policy current, 108
Restraining of inmate, use of physical force for, 143

Restraints, 170, 175–76. *See also* Four-point restraints; Handcuffs; Leg irons
  active counter measures as, 170
  bed restraints, 198
  belts as electronic restraint device, 66
  chains, 194
  description of types of, 137
  extended use of, 70–71, 204–206
  full stationary, 132
  hard, 206
  in-cell, 132
  in isolated area, 201
  medical need for, 199
  medication, 206
  mobile restraint devices, 3
  for movement of inmates, 198
  new and better types of devices for, 89
  policy on, 71
  psychiatric uses, 199
  soft, 206
  should never be used as punishment, 70, 205
  temporary use of, 204
  time limited to necessary amount, 218
  during transfer, 198
  training, 220
  use of, 194–95
Retribution
  as form of punishment, 15
  force must never be used as, 78
Review
  committee for serious incident review, 139
  institutional policies on use of, 48
  and revision of policy, 105
Ricochet-proof ammunition, 89
Riot
  batons as hard intermediate control devices, 66
  control plan, smoke compounds as part of, 184
  condition for use of deadly force, 173
  continuum of force, 180
  helmets, 88
  shields as electronic restraint device, 66
Ripley and Franklin (1982) policy implementation definition, 100

Index

Roadblock operations, 75
Ross, Darrell L., viii
   biographic abstract for, 259
Ross (1997) analysis of Title 42 U.S.C.
   section 1983 prisoner lawsuits, 92
Rotation of
   restrained inmate, 210
   staff absence has potential for excessive
     use of force, 81
Rubber projectiles, 177
Ruffin v. Commonwealth (1871), 18
Rule definition, 9

S

Safeguards to use of force, 207–09
Sam Houston State University, viii
Schwartz, Dr. Jeffery, viii
Searches for individuals departing facility
   under escort, 193–94
Section 1883
   actions, 34–35
   requirements for success of claims, 35
   review of cases filed by inmate plaintiffs,
     92
Securing inmate to a fixed object, 206
Security areas breaching prevention as
   condition of use of deadly force, 173
Security classification of the offender, 194
Security maintenance, use of active counter
   measures without prior approval, 172
Security-type restraint equipment should not
   be used for prolonged time, 70
Self-defense, 26, 27
   force permitted, 204
   permits staff to use active counter
     measures without prior approval, 172
   techniques, active counter measures as, 170
   training requirement, institutional
     policies on, 53
Self-mutilation prevention, active counter
   measures without prior approval, 172
Serious assaults
   on correctional officers, 5
   in housing areas, 5
   warnings absent prior to, 6
Serious body injury, 170

Serious incident review, 139–40
   Committee activities and report for, 140
   report review for, 140
   review committee for, 139
   when held, 139
Severity of punishments as slightly greater
   than the severity of the crime, 16
"Shaming" prisoners, function of "chain
   gangs," 18
Sheets prohibited use, 205
Sheriff, in fugitive pursuit, 75
Shield use, 45–46, 138
"Shocks the conscience" test, 3, 24
Shooting
   escaping inmates, conditions permitted,
     29
   to kill, 160
Show of force as passive counter measures
   as, 169–171
"Significant injury" not necessary for use of
   force to constitute "cruel and unusual
   punishment," 31
Situational, use of force is, 89
Situations in which force is permitted by
   courts, 25
Skin
   disease, 208
   injury, personnel with, 208
Slave of the state, prisoner as, 18
Sleeper holds prohibited, 65
Smoke compounds, 184
"Social contract" perspective on use of
   force, 15
Soft restraints, 170
Software statistical package (SPSS) use in
   analysis of use of force surveys, 41
Solitary confinement as prison punishment,
   17
SORT Team, 74
Special Investigative Supervisor (SIS), 208
Specialized confinement, 44, 59
Specialized restraints, 70–71, 88–89
   institutional policies on techniques, 43–44
Special response teams
   for employing force, 71–75
   institutional policies on use of, 46–47

Spitting or biting, prohibited ways of
  prevention, 205
Staff
  and OC spray, 189
  qualified to use weapons, facility must
    maintain up-to-date list of, 174
  shortages, 58–59
  training of. *See* Training
Standards, 11. *See also* American
    Correctional Association, standards
  ACA update of 1870 Declaration of
    Principles, 20
  determine liability of correctional
    officers, 92–93
  for operating jails and prisons (1977), 21
Standards movement, 20–21
Standardization of language and approaches
  to basic operations value, 20–21
State
  could not be sued for civil damages, 36
  should have sole control over use of
    force, 15
  tort law, 35–36, 34
Statistical tracking system for tracking use-
  of-force incidents, 108
Steel handcuffs, 206
Stingball rounds, 89
Stohr, Mary K., viii
Stohr-Gilmore, Emily, viii
Storage of equipment, 170
Stun guns, 3, 45–46, 218. *See also*
    Electronic stun devices; Kinetic stunning
    device
Stun shield, 72
Suicide prevention, 198
  permits active counter measures without
    prior approval, 172
Supervisor may be liable for actions of
  subordinates, 36
Supervisory incident report review system
  use, 108
Supreme Court. *See* U.S. Supreme Court
Surgical mask, 217
Survey of use-of-force policies
  findings of, 41–59
  value of, 40
Suspected inmate abuse report, 146–47

Suspicion, maximum force should never be
  used on mere, 159
SWAT team, 74. *See also* Forced cell entry

T
Tape, 205, 217
Tasers
  district court finding against use of, 95
  electronic restraint device, 66
  less-than-lethal force weapon, 33
Technology
  applicability in correctional setting, 3
  as element of successful use of force
    program, 88–89
Tennessee v. Garner (1985), 28, 33
Texas
  county jail videotape of abusing inmates,
    113
  Jail Standards Commission requiring
    county formal use-of-force policies,
    113
  study laxity in enforcing correctional
    officer compliance with policies, 11
Toilet use of restrained inmates, 211
Tort, 34
  conditions necessary to prove, 35–36
Towels prohibited use, 205, 217
Training
  chemical agent use, 200
  communication techniques, 220
  confrontation avoidance/use of force
    technique, 220
  cultural diversity, 220
  element of successful use of force
    program, 84–87
  force cannot be used successfully
    without extensive staff, 84
  institutional policies on, 51–52
  mental illness, dealing with, 220
  OC use, 188
  pregnant inmates and restraints, 220
  reporting procedures, 220
  restraint applications, 200, 220
  standards for personnel, 1–2
  time elapse for restraining inmate, 218
  unit, 174
  use of force, 10, 53, 106, 107

About the Authors

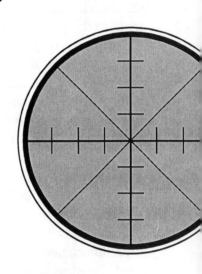

Craig Hemmens

Craig Hemmens teaches in the Department of Criminal Justice Administration at Boise State University, in Boise, Idaho. He has a B.A. from the University of North Carolina, a J.D. from North Carolina Central University School of Law, and a Ph.D. in criminal justice from Sam Houston State University.

He has published more than fifty articles on a variety of criminal justice and legal topics, including corrections law, juvenile justice, and criminal procedure. He has conducted research on inmate perceptions of prison and parole, attitudes of juvenile facility directors, and perceptions of bias in and public opinion of Idaho courts. He is currently conducting research, with his wife and colleague Mary K. Stohr, on the effectiveness of Residential Substance Abuse Treatment (RSAT) programming in Idaho. He is the coauthor of the American Correctional Association book, *From Law to Order: The Theory and Practice of Law and Justice.*

Eugene E. Atherton

Eugene E. Atherton is the warden at the Colorado State Penitentiary, a level-five security, administrative segregation, prison housing 756 inmates. The mission of the Colorado State Penitentiary is to use a highly specialized approach to simultaneously isolate the 4 to 6 percent of Colorado's most high-risk inmates and prepare them for parole, discharge, or return to the general prison population. The Colorado State Penitentiary is the first "super max" type facility to receive American Correctional Association accreditation and special recognition in the form of the American Correctional Association's "Best Practices" award for 1998. Mr. Atherton has acted as a technical assistance consultant for the National Institute of Corrections on a variety of issues and has received special recognition as a contributing editor to the American Correctional Association publication *Guidelines for the Development of A Security Program.*

Mr. Atherton has worked for the Colorado Department of Corrections since 1978. He has served as a case manager, operations lieutenant, housing captain, security major, housing manager, security specialist, and warden. Prior to coming to the Colorado State Penitentiary, Mr. Atherton was warden at the Buena Vista Correctional Facility prison complex. In 1993, he was appointed the security specialist for the Colorado Department of Corrections. In this position, he was responsible for security policy/systems development, emergency management systems, security auditing, security equipment and construction standards, task force leadership on security issues, and new facility planning for a system of 13 facilities and more than 12,000 inmates. He has held leadership positions on such projects as the Colorado State Penitentiary design and activation, design of the San Carlos Correctional Facility (a special needs unit for the chronically mentally ill), and the Sterling Correctional Facility, a prototype prison.

Contributing Authors

Darrell L. Ross

Dr. Darrell Ross is an associate professor of criminal justice at East Carolina University in Greenville, North Carolina. He teaches correctional law, administration, research methods, and institutional corrections. He has taught criminal justice courses for more than twenty years. He is a thirteen-year veteran with the Michigan Department of Corrections, where he accumulated both institutional and probation officer experience, and he has taught for three years in the central correctional academy. His institutional experience was at the State Prison of Southern Michigan, in Jackson, Michigan.

Jeff Maahs

Jeff Maahs is a research associate and Ph.D. candidate in the Division of Criminal Justice at the University of Cincinnati. His research interests include institutional and community corrections and criminological theory. He has published articles on the cost-effectiveness of privatizing prisons, inmate litigation, and the regulation of private security officers.

Travis Pratt

Travis Pratt is a research associate and Ph.D. candidate in the Division of Criminal Justice at the University of Cincinnati. His research interests include criminological theory, sentencing policies, and institutional corrections. He has published articles on correctional privatization and racial disparities in sentencing.